INFLUENCING
HEMINGWAY

INFLUENCING HEMINGWAY

People and Places That Shaped His Life and Work

Nancy W. Sindelar

ROWMAN & LITTLEFIELD
Lanham • Boulder • New York • London

Published by Rowman & Littlefield
A wholly owned subsidary of The Rowman & Littlefield Publishing Group, Inc.
4501 Forbes Boulevard, Suite 200, Lanham, Maryland 20706
www.rowman.com

Unit A, Whitacre Mews, 26-34 Stannary Street, London SE11 4AB

Copyright © 2014 by Rowman & Littlefield

Distributed by NATIONAL BOOK NETWORK

British Library Cataloguing in Publication Information Available

Library of Congress Cataloging-in-Publication Data

Sindelar, Nancy W., 1944–
  Influencing Hemingway : people and places that shaped his life and work /
Nancy W. Sindelar.
      pages cm
  Includes bibliographical references and index.
  ISBN 978-0-8108-9291-0 (cloth : alk. paper) — ISBN 978-1-5381-0240-4
(pbk. : alk. paper) — ISBN 978-0-8108-9292-7 (ebook) 1. Hemingway,
Ernest, 1899-1961—Friends and associates. 2. Hemingway, Ernest, 1899-
1961—Homes and haunts. 3. United States—Intellectual life—20th century.
4. Authors, American—20th century—Biography. I. Title.
  PS3515.E37Z8295 2014
  813'.52—dc23
  [B]   2013049582

♾TM The paper used in this publication meets the minimum requirements of
American National Standard for Information Sciences—Permanence of Paper
for Printed Library Materials, ANSI/NISO Z39.48-1992.

Printed in the United States of America

In memory of Redd Griffin

Contents

Acknowledgments

THE VARIOUS PLACES IN WHICH Ernest Hemingway lived during his lifetime are a testimony to his passion for writing, his love of the outdoors, and his fondness for reading. Though the houses occupy various locations around the world, they have certain similarities. They are filled with books and animal trophies and tend to be in secluded places that promote the concentration needed for writing. A visit to any of Ernest Hemingway's homes creates an opportunity to better understand the author and the people and places that influenced him. Thus, the first acknowledgment is to the various foundations that support and restore the places that were important to Ernest. I am especially grateful to the Ernest Hemingway Foundation of Oak Park as it has provided me as well as others with numerous opportunities to better understand the author and the people and places that were important to him.

While this book focuses on the influences of the people and places, much of the information we have about Ernest's interests and activities comes from photographs and letters. Fortunately for those of us who are interested in the life of Ernest Hemingway, his father was an avid photographer, who took photos of Ernest from his infancy until he left home to join the Red Cross Ambulance Corps. We are fortunate too to have talented people who collect and restore these valued photos. I am particularly grateful to Susan Wrynn and her dedicated interns at the John F. Kennedy Presidential Library and Museum and to Allison Sansone at the Ernest Hemingway Foundation of Oak Park. Together they have provided many of the photos used in this book. I also want to thank Kris Hosbein, who used her considerable skills to bring many of the one-hundred-year-old images back to life.

In addition to the photos, much of the insight into the people who influenced Ernest comes from letters. He was a prolific letter writer and so were his parents, siblings, and many of his friends. His mother also kept detailed memory books that contained photos, early letters, and reflections on Ernest's first eighteen years of life. Whether it was out of love or because of his early fame, many of the letters as well as the memory books have been saved. Again I want to acknowledge the work of the staff at the John F. Kennedy Presidential Library and Museum who gather, restore, and preserve these important documents and also thank Paul Newman for sharing his private collection of reproduced letters exchanged between Ernest and Peter Viertel.

The study of photos and letters as well as the people and places that were important to Ernest shows clear connections between his life experiences and his literary output. As a result, quotations from his works are used to document Ernest's use of his personal experiences in his writing. This use of quotations is a natural outcome of the study of the people and places that shaped his life and work, and acknowledgment and gratitude are given to Simon & Schuster, Inc. for their permission to publish quotations from the following works:

In Our Time
Reprinted with the permission of Scribner Publishing Group from IN OUR TIME by Ernest Hemingway. Copyright © 1925, 1930 by Charles Scribner's Sons; copyright renewed © 1953, 1958 by Ernest Hemingway. All rights reserved.

A Farewell to Arms
Reprinted with the permission of Scribner Publishing Group from A FAREWELL TO ARMS by Ernest Hemingway. Copyright © 1929 by Charles Scribner's Sons. Copyright renewed © 1957 by Ernest Hemingway. All rights reserved.

Acknowledgment and gratitude also are given to Random House UK for their permission to publish quotations from the following works:

"Three-Day Blow," "Indian Camp," "Fathers and Sons," and "Now I Lay Me" taken from *The First Forty-Nine Stories* by Ernest Hemingway, published by Jonathan Cape. Reprinted by permission of The Random House Group Limited

A Farewell to Arms, The Sun Also Rises, Green Hills of Africa, "The Snows of Kilimanjaro," *Death in the Afternoon, To Have and Have Not, For Whom the Bell Tolls, The Old Man and the Sea,* and *A Moveable Feast* by Ernest Hemingway, published by Vintage Books. Reprinted by permission of The Random House Group Limited.

By-line: Selected Articles and Dispatches of Four Decades by Ernest Hemingway, published by Arrow Books. Reprinted by permission of The Random House Group Limited

Finally, I want to acknowledge Stephen Ryan for his guidance in the publication process and thank my family for their interest in the research and writing of this book. Their support and patience has made the production of *Influencing Hemingway: People and Places That Shaped His Life and Work* a fascinating journey into the past and back to places that were important to Ernest.

Chronology

July 21, 1899	Ernest Miller Hemingway is born to Dr. Clarence Hemingway and Grace Hall Hemingway in Oak Park, Illinois.
June 1917	Ernest graduates from Oak Park High School, where he participated in sports, was editor of the school newspaper, and published articles in the literary magazine.
October 1917	Ernest moves to Kansas City and works as a cub reporter for the *Kansas City Star*.
May 1918	Ernest goes to Italy as a Red Cross ambulance driver during World War I.
July 8, 1918	Ernest is injured by a trench mortar shell.
January 1919	Ernest returns to Oak Park.
January–May 1920	Ernest lives in Toronto and writes occasional articles for the *Toronto Star*.
December 1920	Ernest begins writing for the *Cooperative Commonwealth* in Chicago.

September 3, 1921	Ernest marries Hadley Richardson in Horton Bay, Michigan, and then moves with Hadley to Chicago.
December 8, 1921	Ernest and Hadley move to Paris, where Ernest works as a freelance writer for the *Toronto Star*.
July 1923	Ernest takes his first trip to Spain with Robert McAlmon and Bill Bird.
August 1923	*Three Stories and Ten Poems* is published by Robert McAlmon's Contact Editions in Paris.
October 1923	Ernest and Hadley move to Toronto, where Ernest works as a reporter for the *Toronto Star*.
October 10, 1923	John Hadley Nicanor Hemingway (Bumby) is born in Toronto.
January 1924	Ernest, Hadley, and Bumby return to Paris, where Ernest edits the *Transatlantic Review*.
April 1924	*in our time* is published by the Three Mountains Press.
July 1924	Ernest and Hadley take their first trip to Pamplona, Spain, for the Festival of San Fermin.
June–July 1925	Ernest and Hadley, joined by friends, take their second trip to Pamplona, Spain, for the Festival of San Fermin.
October 1925	*In Our Time* is published by Boni and Liveright.
May 1926	*Torrents of Spring* is published by Scribner's.
October 1926	*The Sun Also Rises* is published by Scribner's.

April 14, 1927	Hadley divorces Ernest.
May 10, 1927	Ernest marries Pauline Pfeiffer in Paris.
October 1927	*Men without Women* is published by Scribner's.
March 1928	Ernest and Pauline move to Key West, Florida.
June 28, 1928	Patrick Hemingway is born in Kansas City.
December 6, 1928	Clarence Hemingway dies of a self-inflicted gunshot wound in Oak Park, Illinois.
September 1929	*A Farewell to Arms* is published by Scribner's.
November 12, 1931	Gregory Hemingway is born in Kansas City.
September 1932	*Death in the Afternoon* is published by Scribner's.
August 1933	Ernest and Pauline go on an African safari.
May 1934	Ernest orders the *Pilar* from the Wheeler Shipyard in Brooklyn.
October 1935	*Green Hills of Africa* is published by Scribner's.
November 1936	Ernest is hired by NANA (North American Newspaper Alliance) as a war correspondent to cover the Spanish Civil War.
October 1937	*To Have and Have Not* is published by Scribner's.
April 1939	Ernest moves to Finca Vigia near Havana with Martha Gellhorn. After their marriage, Ernest purchases the property.

October 1940	*For Whom the Bell Tolls* is published by Scribner's.
November 4, 1940	Pauline divorces Ernest.
November 21, 1940	Ernest marries Martha Gellhorn in Cheyenne, Wyoming.
February–May 1941	Ernest and Martha travel to China to cover the Sino-Japanese War.
January 1942–April 1944	Ernest lives in Cuba and periodically patrols Cuban waters for German submarines.
May 1944	Ernest is hired by *Collier's* as a war correspondent to cover World War II.
December 21, 1945	Ernest divorces Martha.
March 14, 1946	Ernest marries Mary Welsh in Havana.
June 13, 1947	Ernest is awarded the Bronze Star at the U.S. Embassy in Havana for "meritorious service as a war correspondent" in France and Germany.
October 1948	Ernest and Mary Hemingway travel to Italy, where Ernest meets Adriana Ivancich.
September 1950	*Across the River and into the Trees* is published by Scribner's.
June 28, 1951	Grace Hall Hemingway dies in Memphis, Tennessee.
September 1952	*The Old Man and the Sea* is published by Scribner's.
May 1953	Ernest is awarded the Pulitzer Prize for *The Old Man and the Sea*.
June 1953–March 1954	Ernest and Mary travel to Spain and Africa. In Africa, they survive two plane crashes.

October 1954	Ernest is awarded the Nobel Prize in Literature.
December 1957	In Cuba, Ernest begins work on *A Moveable Feast*.
January 1959	Fidel Castro takes over the governing of Cuba. Batista flees the country. Ernest decides to purchase a house in Ketchum, Idaho.
Summer 1959	Ernest and Mary travel to Spain. Ernest begins work on *The Dangerous Summer*.
May 1960	After extensive editing *The Dangerous Summer* is published in *Life*. The book, *Dangerous Summer*, is published posthumously by Scribner's.
November 1960	Ernest begins treatments for depression at the Mayo Clinic in Rochester, Minnesota.
July 2, 1961	Ernest dies of a self-inflicted gunshot wound in Ketchum, Idaho.

Introduction

FOR A LONG TIME I'VE ADMIRED the Hemingway Code as means for living an active life and facing the challenges life throws in one's path. As a teacher of literature, I found that my students could embrace the Code too. Living a life filled with action and ritual, not engaging in self-pity, and trying to exhibit grace under pressure was a philosophy of life most could accept regardless of their age.

As a former English teacher at Hemingway's alma mater, Oak Park and River Forest High School, I first explored Ernest's high school years as a means of engaging students in his novels. My students were quick to view Hemingway as a legendary man who courted life-threatening adventures and glamorous friends while writing articles, novels, and short stories that captivated the world. However, many felt that their own lives paled in comparison to his and that being in school was often "just boring."

My students' attitudes inspired me to do some research on Ernest's life as a high school student. I studied his yearbooks and his high school writing and even met some of his former teachers. Turns out young Hemingway was a good student, an involved athlete, and an aspiring writer. Together, my students and I learned that the man who became an international sports legend and literary figure also was an avid reader, a high school athlete, the editor of the school's newspaper, a contributor to the literary magazine and that he played the cello in the school's orchestra and participated in the school play. Clearly, he was just as involved with life as a teenager as he was as an adult. This information helped make Hemingway real to students and showed them that involvement in school could lead to a life of action and adventure.

Living in the Oak Park River Forest area for more than thirty years also gave me an understanding of the culture in which Ernest was raised. Ernest's parents valued education and lived by a clearly defined set of Christian principles. Oak Park then—as it is now—was a community focused on high educational expectations, and the strict Protestantism of Ernest's family and the religious influences of Wheaton College can still be found in pockets of the western suburbs of Chicago.

Because much of my youth was spent racing sailboats to Mackinac Island in northern Michigan, I also had an appreciation for Walloon Lake and the "summer people" of northern Michigan. During his summers in Michigan, Ernest learned to hunt and fish and gained a sense of self-reliance and confidence that influenced many of his decisions. Knowing the rugged isolation of northern Michigan, I came to believe that Ernest's often-maligned mother was a courageous enabler, who managed a family of six children in a spartan, rugged environment.

Having lived in Switzerland and having spent time in France, I could also see how a boy from Oak Park could be energized and transformed by the people, the food, and the freedom of Paris during the 1920s, and equally thrilled with the opportunities to ski and sled in the mountains of Switzerland. Similarly, as skiing and hunting drew Ernest to Sun Valley, Idaho, I too was attracted to the resort and knew well the celebrity atmosphere of the Sun Valley Lodge and the mountain comfort of the Christiana Inn and Trail Creek Cabin that Ernest experienced later in life.

My first trip to Cuba was summer 2011. I had been asked to make a presentation at the thirteenth International Ernest Hemingway Colloquium, a gathering of international scholars whose ideas, research, and presentations created an interesting and controversial picture of the writer's life and legend. After only a few days in Havana, it was clear to me why he was attracted to Cuba and why the twenty-two years he spent there was the longest period of time he lived anywhere. The people were charming, honest, and friendly; the climate and culture were warm and exotic; and the island was surrounded by beautiful waters and opportunities for world-class fishing.

Ernest liked Cuba, and the Cubans liked him. At the colloquium Cuban scholars spoke with passion regarding the importance of the Cuban waters to the content of his novels, his role in patrolling the waters for submarines during World War II, and his relationship with Fidel Castro, another avid fisherman. But Ernest's popularity was not just with the intellectuals and scholars; it seemed to run throughout the country and was particularly visible among the Cuban fishermen.

For many years, Ernest spent time in the fishing village of Cojimar. He kept his boat in the harbor there, frequented the local restaurants and bars in the town, and used the town and the neighboring waters as the setting and inspiration for *Old Man and the Sea*. When he died, the local Cojimar fishermen honored his memory by melting, among other things, the propellers of their boats to create a bronze bust of the author. The bust of Hemingway overlooks the harbor, is situated under a locally constructed classical dome, and is one of the most significant pieces of art and architecture in the town.

My colloquium presentation focused on the people and places that influenced Ernest from his birth to his graduation from high school and was documented and illustrated by stories about the influences of his grandparents, parents, and teachers and punctuated with photos of his birthplace and boyhood homes, his summers in northern Michigan, and his interests and scholarship while in high school. The presentation had no political bias, no particular prejudice about the writer or the legend, and was silent regarding the impact of the author's four wives and various extramarital relationships. It was the story of a boy and his family.

What became significant was the impact of Ernest's early years on the rest of his life—how a little boy, fishing with his father, developed a lifelong love for the sea and sportfishing, and how his mother, who often has been viewed as a controlling shrew, could be viewed as a caring woman who nurtured a lifelong passion for fishing and the outdoors in her son.

As the colloquium progressed, it became clear that the boy from Oak Park, Illinois, grew to be not only a great writer but a captivating and complex legend. Not only was he an iconic American author, but scholars from around the world claimed him as their own. Spending time in Cuba, seeing Hemingway's house, his clothes, his boat, his typewriter and visiting his favorite bars and restaurants yielded a deeper understanding of how the people and events in his early life shaped the thinking and actions of both the writer and the legend.

After more trips to Cuba and additional research, *Influencing Hemingway* was written as a modest attempt to document how Ernest Hemingway's early years and the people and places Ernest was drawn to in his adult life contributed to his thoughts, actions, and writing. Completing the research for *Influencing Hemingway* has been a wonderful journey into the lives of people as well as to the places that were loved by an extraordinary writer and legend. Hopefully the reader will learn how the people and places that were important to Ernest not only nourished and stimulated him as a person, but also enabled both the writer and the legend to live the life of action and ritual that he captured so effectively in portrayal of his Code Heroes.

Chapter One

Early Influences: People, Places, and Lifelong Pursuits

It is the child who makes the man, and no man exists who was not made by the child he once was.

—Maria Montessori[1]

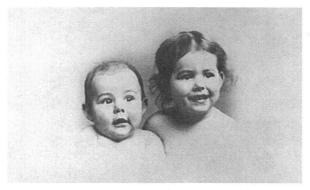

Ernest Hemingway at six months with his sister Marcelline, age two. *Ernest Hemingway Foundation of Oak Park*

ERNEST HEMINGWAY'S LIFE AND WORK SUPPORTS the truism of psychology that parent-child interactions have an enormous impact on a child's attitudes, values, and personality. Since children have no attitudes as infants, they start their lives by absorbing uncritically what their parents say and do. Parents influence their children's interests and activities by encouraging hobbies and vocations and by the total set of experiences they provide to their family. Once these parental-based attitudes are acquired, they influence the way in which the child reacts to subsequent information, while the emotional relationship that develops between parents and the child intensifies the effect of any parental rewards or punishments.

Powerful as the parental impact is, it is limited. As children grow older, they interact with more people, have a broader range of experience on which to base their attitudes, and are increasingly impressed by what they read, what they experience, and the new people with whom they interact. However, though the correlations between attitudes of parents and children lessen with time, they are still significant.

Many of the people, places, and activities Ernest Hemingway was drawn to in his adult life were the result of childhood interests nurtured by his parents and grandparents. Both of his grandfathers were veterans of the Civil War, and his paternal grandfather, Anson Hemingway, introduced his grandson to the concept that war was a venue for men to display courage and honor. His father, Dr. Clarence Hemingway, taught his son the skills of hunting and fishing. Because of these early influences, it's not surprising that Ernest Hemingway left home and forsook a college education to become a Red Cross volunteer in Italy during World War I, was actively involved in the Spanish Civil War and World War II, and found time to hunt in Africa and fish in the waters of the Gulf Stream when he was not engaged in the craft of writing.

Similarly it's not surprising that Ernest eventually was drawn to Cuba and lived there for twenty-two years, longer than in any other place. It was a perfect place for him. He could practice his well-honed ritual of writing in the morning and then engage in world-class fishing in the afternoon.

From the time Ernest was six weeks old to the time he left for his first job at the *Kansas City Star*, he spent every summer in northern Michigan, fishing. Like other "summer people," the

Hemingways were lured to Michigan by the cool northern air, the natural beauty of the lakes and forests, and the opportunities for hunting and fishing. The family summer home, Windemere, was located on Walloon Lake, and each summer the family left Oak Park, Illinois, and took a lake steamer three hundred miles north on Lake Michigan to Harbor Springs, Michigan. From there, they traveled by train to Petoskey and then to Walloon Village and again by boat to the house on Walloon Lake.

The only exception to this travel plan was made the summer of 1917 when only the Hemingway girls traveled to Walloon Lake by steamer. Ernest, his father and mother, and young Leister made the summer journey in the family car, a Ford Model T touring car. The 487-mile journey took five days. The family camped in tents at night and brought along a saw so that Ernest could cut branches to provide traction for the car on the sandy roads of northern Michigan.

The adventurous summer trips reflect the value the Hemingway family placed on balancing life in suburban Oak Park with the natural world found in Michigan. Dr. Clarence Hemingway, Ernest's father, loved to fish, was an excellent marksman, and trained his son to not only love and respect nature, but also become skilled as a fisherman and marksman. Grace Hall Hemingway, Ernest's mother, enabled her son's interests by traveling with her six children to the remote and isolated Walloon Lake. Unlike most women of her day, Grace fished, engaged in target shooting with her own .22, and promoted a family culture that embraced the out-of-doors. Though much has been written about Ernest's dislike of his mother, the early years indicate that she promoted a life, especially during the summer months, that enabled her son to learn and eventually excel in sports that were meaningful to him his entire life.

For Ernest Hemingway fishing became a lifelong ritual, passion, and source of pleasure. Dr. Hemingway introduced Ernest to fishing during the summers in Michigan, and when he was eleven, his mother took him by train and steamer to Cape Cod and Nantucket, where he first experienced salt water and fishing for mackerel and sea bass.

Later in life his love of fishing drew him to Key West, Florida, and then eventually to Cuba. Even shortly before his death in Idaho in 1961, Hemingway wrote from the Mayo Clinic in Rochester, Minnesota, to the young son of his Idaho physician, saying, "Saw some good bass jumping in the river. I never knew anything about

Grace Hall Hemingway showing Ernest and his sisters, Marcelline and Ursula, the seven-pound pike she has caught. Note that Ernest is dressed as a Native American Indian. *Ernest Hemingway Foundation of Oak Park*

the upper Mississippi before and it is really a very beautiful country and there are plenty of pheasants and ducks in the fall."[2]

Dr. Hemingway's love of fishing and hunting not only influenced his son's lifelong love of fishing, it eventually permeated his son's writing. During those early summers, Ernest and his father fished for trout in the cold, clear waters of northern Michigan using worms and hand-tied flies. The memories of these times with his father would later appear in the Nick Adams stories.

In "Indian Camp," young Nick is returning home with his doctor father. "They were seated in the boat, Nick in the stern, his father rowing. The sun was coming up over the hills. A bass jumped, making a circle in the water. Nick trailed his hand in the water. It felt warm in the sharp chill of the morning."[3] As they are rowing across the lake, Nick asks his father if dying is hard. His father says, "No, I think it's pretty easy," and Nick concludes that "in the early morning on the lake sitting in the stern of the boat with his father rowing, . . . he would never die." [4]

From the Nick Adams stories to the major novels, readers find Hemingway's characters taking comfort in the out-of-doors as well as respecting and meeting the challenges presented by the natural world. Even years later, battling the gloom of depression, Ernest would reminisce about the fishermen in Paris, saying in *A Moveable Feast* that "with the fishermen and the life on the river, the beautiful barges with their own life on board . . . the great elms on the stone banks of the river . . . I could never be lonely along the river."[5]

In addition to fishing, Ernest's father taught him to hunt. The Indians of northern Michigan had great respect, both as a physician and as a marksman, for Dr. Hemingway, whom they called Ne-teck-ta-la or Eagle Eye. Ernest and his family engaged in the ritual of target practice at Walloon Lake, but also hunted for ducks and other small game. Memories of his father and life at Walloon Lake would be remembered in "Fathers and Sons," as Ernest would later write,

> Someone has to give you your first gun or the opportunity to get it and use it, and you have to live where there is game or fish if you are to learn about them, and now, at thirty-eight, he loved to fish and to shoot exactly as much as when he first had gone with his father. It was a passion that had never slackened and he was very grateful to his father for bringing him to know it.[6]

Ernest and his father, Dr. Clarence Hemingway, fishing on Walloon Lake. The boat, *Marcelline of Windemere*, was named after Ernest's sister. *Ernest Hemingway Foundation of Oak Park*

Ernest circa 1917 fishing on Walloon Lake. *Ernest Hemingway Foundation of Oak Park*

The Hemingways arrive in Michigan by car in 1917. Ernest is wearing his high school "letter sweater." *Ernest Hemingway Foundation of Oak Park*

He would go on to say that "his father came back to him in the fall of the year, or in the early spring when there had been jacksnipe on the prairie, or when he saw shocks of corn, or when he saw a lake or . . . heard wild geese, or in a duck blind."[7]

The early fishing and hunting experiences gave Ernest the interest and skills to pursue hunting and fishing his entire life and eventually contributed to the creation of the Hemingway legend. As a young writer Ernest supplemented his income with articles and short stories published in *Esquire*, *Holiday*, and *Scribner's*. In addition to creating the image of Ernest as a masculine, adventurous outdoorsman, the articles provided income that often was spent on hunting and fishing trips.

Certainly, an early contribution to the legend was the 1934 three-month safari in Kenya Colony, East Africa, where he hunted lions and rhinoceroses. When he disembarked from the SS *Paris* in New York City on his return to the United States, his adventures were widely publicized. Ernest spoke of the lion as a "fine animal . . . [that] is not afraid or stupid" and was quoted by the *New York Times*, enthusiastically saying he was returning home "to make enough money to return to East Africa."[8] As time progressed, he continued to cultivate a masculine, authoritative image of himself as the big game hunter and sports fisherman, augmented with photographs of himself with fallen lions or four-hundred-pound marlin.

During the summers in northern Michigan, young Ernest also began the initiation into what later became the Hemingway Code—a set of actions and rituals that enable an individual to endure the difficulties life throws in his way, realizing that he ultimately will lose because of his own mortality. A Code Hero "offers up and exemplifies certain principles of honor, courage, and endurance which in a life of tension and pain make a man a man."[9] Ernest's Code Heroes play the game of life honestly and passionately in spite of the knowledge that death is the ultimate end. They maintain free will and individualism, never weakly allowing social convention to prevent "beautiful adventures" or acts of bravery. When the time comes, the Code Heroes face death with dignity, enduring physical and emotional pain in silence.

A key element to living by the Code is admitting the truth of Nada, that is, that no external source outside of oneself can provide meaning or purpose. This awareness involves facing death without hope of an afterlife, which the Code Hero considers more brave than cowering behind false religious hopes. Ultimately, the Code involves living a life filled with action and ritual as well as a life in which the Code Hero faces death with grace and dignity and without self-pity.

Ernest's initiation to the Code began in northern Michigan when Dr. Hemingway took his young son along as he provided pro bono medical services and attended to injured Indians, squaws in childbirth, and individuals in a variety of life-threatening situations. The memories of these times with his father also would later appear in the Nick Adams stories.

In "Indian Camp," young Nick is with his father on a medical mission to deliver a baby. A squaw's been in labor for two days, and Nick observes his father perform a Cesarean section with a jackknife sterilized in a basin of boiled water. Nick recalls that "his father picked up the baby and slapped it to make it breathe and handed it to the old woman. 'See, it's a boy, Nick.'"[10]

By accompanying his father, Ernest observed early in life how a variety of men and women faced pain, illness, and death. Before he was even in high school, he learned how some people engage in self-pity, others take comfort in religion, and others embrace what he would later call "grace under pressure."

By the age of six, young Ernest also confronted the realities of sickness and death when his maternal grandfather, Ernest "Abba" Hall, died as the result of the kidney ailment called Bright's disease. Ernest lived with Abba from the day he was born and observed Abba's illness and then his death. As was the custom of the time, Abba was waked in the Oak Park Avenue birthplace home. Years later Ernest would have Frederic Henry comment on Catherine Barkley's death after an unsuccessful Cesarean section in *A Farewell to Arms*, saying, "It was like saying good-bye to a statue."[11] One can only wonder if these words weren't influenced by young Ernest's memory of the laid-out corpse of his grandfather, Abba.

Ernest's paternal grandfather, Anson Hemingway, influenced his grandson too. Anson served in the Civil War in the Seventy-second

Ernest (Abba) Hall's bedroom in the birthplace home at 339 N. Oak Park Avenue, Oak Park, Illinois. Abba died from Bright's disease in this room when Ernest was five years old. As was the custom, he was waked at home. *Ernest Hemingway Foundation of Oak Park*

Anson and Adelaide Hemingway, Memorial Day, 1915, outside the boyhood home at 600 N. Kenilworth, Oak Park, Illinois. Anson is proudly wearing his Civil War uniform and medals. *Ernest Hemingway Foundation of Oak Park*

Illinois Infantry Division. He enlisted in 1862 when he was only seventeen was commissioned as a first lieutenant in 1864 and honorably discharged in 1866. He fought in the battle at Vicksburg and wrote in his war journal that "this place is very strongly fortified and it will cost a man a life to take it—but it must fall. We must take it."[12] Anson's half brothers also fought in the Civil War. Only Anson returned alive.

As Ernest grew up, he observed Grandfather Anson proudly wearing his Civil War uniform, displaying his medals, and marching with his comrades in the yearly Oak Park Memorial Day parades. From his grandfather Anson, Ernest learned that war was an event men could be drawn to as a venue for displaying the virtues of honor and courage, virtues that Ernest would later display as a Red Cross volunteer in Italy during World War I and later debate in his novels *A Farewell to Arms* and *For Whom the Bell Tolls*.

Ernest Hemingway was born at home in Oak Park, Illinois, on July 21, 1899. Ernest's birthplace home originally was built in the 1880s by his maternal grandfather and grandmother, Ernest (Abba) and Caroline Hall. When Caroline Hall became ill with cancer, young Dr. Clarence Hemingway, who lived across the street, assisted the family's physician, Dr. William Lewis, in providing medical treatment.

In the course of his medical visits, Clarence met Ernest and Caroline's daughter, Grace, whom he eventually courted and married. After Caroline's death, Dr. Hemingway married Grace and moved across the street and lived with his new wife and her father. Dr. Hemingway, who became chief of obstetrics at Oak Park Hospital, maintained an office in the home, where he saw patients. His office contained Ball jars with snakes, toads, and salamanders bleached white in alcohol as well as specimen jars containing an appendix and a human fetus. In the closet was a skeleton the family eventually named "Suzy-Bone-a-Part."

The Oak Park Avenue house was typical of the era in that it was situated on one of the early developed streets that ran perpendicularly to Lake Street, the town's main street. The Hall-Hemingway house, like other early Oak Park houses, was built close to Lake Street, which was the center of town because it also was the location of the train, which connected suburban Oak Park to Chicago.

The birthplace home was a Queen Anne–style home, popular at the time, and featured the distinctive characteristics of the American Queen Anne architecture, including an asymmetrical façade with

The birthplace home of Ernest Hemingway at 339 N. Oak Park Avenue, Oak Park, Illinois. *Ernest Hemingway Foundation of Oak Park*

The parlor and library of the birthplace home. The parlor contains Grace's piano; the library holds literary classics that Ernest was encouraged to read. *Ernest Hemingway Foundation of Oak Park*

differing wall textures, a dominant turret, and a south-facing porch with painted balustrades. Despite some rather negative descriptions of Oak Park as a community of "repressive four-square enclosures . . . bulwarked against nature and the cold," the birthplace home was a warm, inviting home filled with books, music, and loving, well-disciplined people.[13]

The first-floor library contained books that Ernest and his siblings were encouraged to read. Marcelline, Ernest's older sister, has recalled that one spring when Ernest and she were home from school together with the mumps, they read classics from the family library, including all of Shakespeare's tragedies and comedies and all of Thackeray's *Vanity Fair*.

The parlor contained Grace's piano and was the site for her voice lessons and family concerts. As Ernest was growing up, Grace gave music lessons, and Ernest sometimes had to defend the dramatic edge of his mother's singing, saying he knew people didn't like her singing, "but I remember her singing to me when I was little."[14] The family also had a small "orchestra." Dr. Hemingway played his cornet, Ernest played the cello, Marcelline played the violin, Uncle Tyley played the flute, and Grace or Sunny played the piano. Their repertoire included hymns, songs from Gilbert and Sullivan musicals, and the simpler parts of famous sonatas.

Clearly, the inhabitants of the Oak Park Avenue house were supportive and loving of young Ernest. His father was fascinated with science and engaged in the hobbies of taxidermy and photography when not hunting, fishing, or practicing medicine. Ernest often accompanied his father to the turreted attic room to view his father's specimen jars and the Indian artifacts collected there. Clarence was proud of his son's interest in science and the fact that he could read and name the contents of the jars at an early age.

Dr. Hemingway's parental devotion was strict, stern, and religious. When Ernest turned sixteen, he wrote, "I am so pleased and proud you have grown to be such a fine big manly fellow and will trust your development will continue symmetrical and in harmony with our highest Christian Ideals."[15] As a strict Congregationalist, he disapproved of drinking, dancing, smoking, and card playing. Though Grace seems to have earned a reputation for being the repressive parent, it was she who interceded for her children to attend school dances.

Grace's maternal instincts and love for her son appear in numerous notes and letters. She kept a series of five memory book albums from Ernest's birth until he was eighteen. When he was an infant she noted, "He is contented to sleep with Mama and lunches all night."[16] When he was a toddler and she asked what he was afraid of, he said, "'Fraid a nothing!"[17] She also reported that once while singing "Onward Christian Soldier" to him, he said that when he was a big boy, he didn't want to be an Onward Christian Soldier, but wanted to "go with Dad to hunt lions and wolves."[18]

From Ernest's earliest days, Dr. and Mrs. Hemingway nurtured values that encouraged high moral principles, a strong work ethic, scholarship, and an involvement with outdoor activities that placed emphasis on physical endurance and courage. "'Fraid of nothing!" eventually became a standard of behavior for Ernest, which he later embraced regardless of the challenge or the adversity.

The birthplace home also contained rooms for older role models. Ernest called his maternal grandfather Abba Bear. After meals Abba would retreat to the library, shut the doors, and smoke a cigar, but he too was a loving supporter of young Ernest, saying, "This boy is going to be heard from someday. If he uses his imagination for good purposes, he'll be famous."[19]

Then there was the guest room for Uncle Tyley Hancock, a traveling salesman, who would appear after sales trips and entertain young Ernest with stories of his voyage around the Horn with his sea captain father. Uncle Tyley's exploits no doubt fueled Ernest's interests in adventure and perhaps alcohol, as Dr. Hemingway on more than one occasion had to rescue Uncle Tyley from the nearby Forest Park taverns.

Finally, there were occasional but very special visits from Uncle Willoughby Hemingway, a medical doctor and missionary in China. He too carried the Hemingway gene for courage and adventure. As a medical student he had watched his own appendectomy in mirrors hung over the operation table. Then he traveled to Mongolia and spent much of his life in China. When he returned to the States, he brought his two little Chinese-speaking daughters and stories of an abandoned Chinese orphan whom the Hemingways supported in a mission school.

After Abba's death, Grace Hall Hemingway used her inheritance to build her dream home, where Ernest lived until his departure to Kansas City after graduation from high school. The 1906 "boyhood home" reflects the prairie-style influence of neighbor and architect Frank Lloyd Wright, who lived in Oak Park from 1889 to 1909. Believing that the architecture of Queen Anne–style homes was too vertical and ornate to blend in with the flat prairie landscape of the Midwest, Wright began designing houses with low horizontal lines and more open interior spaces. These homes were called *prairie-style* after Wright's 1901 *Ladies' Home Journal* plan titled "A Home in a Prairie Town."

Grace Hall Hemingway designed her 4,500-square-foot dream home in collaboration with architect H. Fiddelke. The house exhibits the typical prairie-style features of overhanging eaves and a more horizontal feeling. Typical of the first prairie houses, the boyhood home is stucco with wood trim.

In preparation for the move to the new house, Grace got rid of her parents' old Victorian furniture and much of the clutter that had accumulated in the house that she had lived in since she was fifteen. She moved only her mother's oil paintings, her father's books, and her piano.

Ernest observed the purge and later recalled in "Now I Lay Me,"

> I remembered, after my grandfather died we moved away from that house to a new house designed and built by my mother. Many things that were not to be moved were burned in the backyard. And I remember those jars from the attic being thrown into the fire, and how they popped in the heat and the fire flamed up from the alcohol. I remember the snakes burning in the fire in the backyard.[20]

When Ernest was six years old, his family moved to the new home. He attended the local public elementary school, Oliver Wendell Holmes, and then Oak Park High School. For some strange reason, Grace wanted to raise Ernest and Marcelline as twins, and they began school together. She held Marcelline back, and as a result Ernest began school at age seven and Marcelline at age eight and one-half. Despite the difference in their ages, they progressed through elementary and high school together.

As an adolescent, Ernest had the opportunity to experiment with a variety of activities. He was fortunate to attend Oak Park High School, a large comprehensive high school that offered a variety of

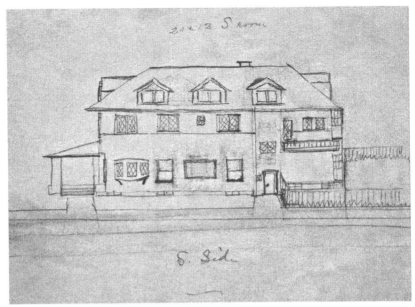

Grace Hall Hemingway's sketch of her future "dream home" at 600 N. Ke-nilworth, Oak Park, Illinois. *Ernest Hemingway Foundation of Oak Park*

Ernest, age six, standing with his sisters, Marcelline and Ursula, in front of the newly built 4,500-square-foot "dream home" at 600 N. Kenilworth Avenue, Oak Park, Illinois. *Ernest Hemingway Foundation of Oak Park*

Ernest Hemingway with the varsity football team at Oak Park High School. *Courtesy Oak Park Public Library, Oak Park, Illinois*

Ernest Hemingway with the swim team at Oak Park High School. *Courtesy Oak Park Public Library, Oak Park, Illinois*

Ernest Hemingway with the track team at Oak Park High School. *Courtesy Oak Park Public Library, Oak Park, Illinois*

Ernest Hemingway in the class play, *Beau Brummel,* at Oak Park High School. *Courtesy Oak Park Public Library, Oak Park, Illinois*

extracurricular activities. In addition to football, swimming, track, and rifle club, Ernest participated in school plays, played the cello in the school orchestra, and became a published author as a result of his participation in *Trapeze,* the school newspaper, and *Tabula,* the school's literary magazine. When he was fourteen, he also convinced his father to pay for a series of boxing lessons at a Chicago gym.

Though Ernest eventually dropped his interests in theater and performance music, he used his sense of drama to later embellish the legendary aspects of his life and career and enjoyed listening to music his entire life. His high school writing experiences not only taught him the craft of journalistic writing, but paved the way for jobs as a cub reporter at the *Kansas City Star,* a foreign correspondent for the *Toronto Star,* and later as a war correspondent for the North American Newspaper Alliance (NANA) and *Collier's.*

Ernest's high school writing efforts reflect his adolescent sense of humor, his interest in sports, and his love of nature and the out-of-doors. As a contributor to the newspaper, he poked fun at his commercial law teacher, saying, "Mr. Larson entertained his seventh period Commercial Law class at a slumber party last Tuesday."[21] As the sports writer for the paper, he detailed a football game, saying, "Hemingway went over for the first touchdown by way of the Lake Street 'L.'"[22] As the author of the short story "Judgment of Manitou," he reflected on the out-of-doors life learned from summers in Michigan by developing a conflict between two Canadian trappers, Dick Haywood and his half-French and half-Cree partner, Pierre. Pierre suspects that Dick has stolen his wallet and plots revenge in a murder in which Dick is caught in a bear trap and killed by timber wolves. As the story progresses, Pierre is lying on a cot in their cabin and sees a red squirrel chewing on the wallet. Pierre rushes out of the cabin to save his friend only to find bloody snow and ravens picking at the shapeless something that had once been his partner. Pierre then becomes the victim of his own plot as he steps into the open bear trap that Haywood had come to tend. Realizing it's the judgment of Manitou, Pierre kills himself with his own rifle.

Ernest's publication efforts were encouraged by his high school journalism teacher, Fannie Biggs. Miss Biggs conducted her journalism classroom as though it were a newspaper room, with rotating editors and daily assignments of news stories, sports, and advertising. Miss Biggs taught her students there were three criteria for a good article: "Tell your whole story in the first paragraph; develop details in relation to their importance; leave the least important things till the end because the editor may have to cut."[23] Ernest's first article, "Concert a Success," appeared in the *Trapeze* January 20, 1916, and reported on a performance the Chicago Symphony Orchestra had given in Oak Park.

While the extracurricular activities in writing and sports offered by the high school nurtured the beginnings of a disciplined life of action and ritual, the high school's academic curriculum extended and developed Ernest's interest and understanding of literary classics. Though the Hemingway family encouraged cultural literacy with trips to Chicago's Art Institute, the Field Museum, symphony concerts, and operas and maintained a family library stocked with literary classics, the high school English curriculum developed his understanding of great English authors, including Chaucer, Spenser, Milton, Pope, Wordsworth, Keats, Browning, and Arnold.

While Franklin's *Autobiography* was required reading in freshman English, it appears Ernest had no formal course in American literature. Ernest's admiration for Ring Lardner, whom he imitated in articles for the *Trapeze*, was probably acquired from reading Lardner's "In the Wake of the News," a column in the *Chicago Tribune*, while his reading of Stephen Crane's *Red Badge of Courage* and Twain's *Life on the Mississippi* was a result of his habit of extending his reading list by loading up on books from the local Oak Park Public Library for summer reading at Walloon Lake. Due to a variety of influences, it's clear that from an early age Ernest was an avid reader of European and American authors, allowing him to one day draw a line in the literary sand by saying, "All American literature begins with *Huckleberry Finn*."[24]

The word *adolescence* comes from the Latin verb *adolescere*, which means "to grow" or "to grow into maturity." Certainly, the high school experiences allowed Ernest, the teenager, to evaluate his personal assets and liabilities and learn how to use them to achieve a clearer concept of who and what he wanted to be and become. At Oak Park High School he was able to work through the transitional period between childhood and adulthood by exploring a variety of athletic activities, engaging in challenging curriculum, and trying out an occupation that would become for him a lifetime endeavor.

Ernest's parents and grandparents were college educated, and the family's plan was for both Ernest and his older sister, Marcelline, to continue their educations at Oberlin College. Marcelline and Ernest state in the high school yearbook that they will attend Oberlin and the University of Illinois, respectively; however, Ernest rejected the family tradition and, after a summer at Walloon Lake, headed to Kansas City as a cub reporter for the *Kansas City Star*. Though Ernest's family was disappointed in his decision to not attend college, it appears that the support Ernest received from his parents and grandparents coupled with his high school experiences gave Ernest the positive self-concept and the confidence, courage, and motivation to believe he was smart enough and good enough to break with family tradition and be a writer without the benefit of a university degree.

While the summer of 1917 was marked by conflict regarding Ernest's future, to some extent resolution came when Uncle (Alfred) Tyler Hemingway arranged an October interview for Ernest at the *Kansas City Star*. After the interview with Henry Haskell,

MADELEINE HANCOCK

Glee Club (3) (4); Opera (3); Atalanta (2) (3) (4); French Club (3) (4); Girls' Club (3) (4).

"As smooth as the business side of a banana peel."

WARD BELMONT

WILBUR HAUPT

Glee Club (2) (3); Opera (2); German Play (2); Athletic Association (4); Boys' High school Club (3) (4); Hanna Club (3).

"Cheeks like roses."

ILLINOIS

ERNEST HEMINGWAY

Class Prophet; Orchestra (1) (2) (3); Trapeze Staff (3), Editor (4); Class Play; Burke Club (3) (4); Athletic Association (1) (2) (4); Boys' High School Club (3) (4); Hanna Club (1) (3) (4); Boys' Rifle Club (1) (2) (3); Major Football (4); Minor Football (2) (3); Track Manager (4); Swimming (4).

"None are to be found more clever than Ernie."

ILLINOIS

MARCELLINE HEMINGWAY

Commencement Speaker; Orchestra (1) (2) (3) (4); Glee Club (3) (4); Tabula Board (4); Trapeze Staff (3), Editor (4); Opera (1) (2) (3); Atalanta (1) (2) (3) (4); Girls' Rifle Club (2) (3) (4); Commercial Club (4); Drama Club (3) (4); Girls' Club (3), Council (4); Story Club (3).

"I'd give a dollar for one of your dimples, Marc."

OBERLIN

Ernest Hemingway's graduation photo and yearbook entry, Oak Park High School, 1917. *Courtesy Oak Park Public Library, Oak Park, Illinois*

Uncle Tyler's Oberlin classmate and the chief editorial writer for
the *Kansas City Star*, Ernest was put on a thirty-day trial period at
$15 a week.

Ernest initially spent four days with Uncle Tyler and Aunt Ara-
bella in Kansas City, but he quickly made arrangements to move to
Miss Haines's boardinghouse on Warrick Avenue. Then in November 1917, when he was offered and accepted a regular reporter's
job, he began sharing a $2.50 a week apartment at 3516 Agnes
Street with Carl Edgar, whom he'd met that summer in Michigan.
Though Ernest wrote to his parents that he and Carl had a "nice big
room with easy chairs and a table, dresser and sleeping porch with
two double beds," he omitted the fact that the porch was so cold he
had to wear his coat to bed.[25]

Much has been written about the influence of the seven-month
apprenticeship at the *Kansas City Star* on Ernest's writing. The *Kansas City Star's* style manual, which promoted the use of short sentences, short paragraphs, and vigorous English, is often credited with
influencing the author's style. Ernest, himself, would one day say
that the 110 rules contained on the style sheet were "the best rules I
ever learned for the business of writing. I've never forgotten them."[26]

The months in Kansas City also provided the opportunities for
Ernest to broaden his personal experiences beyond those of Oak
Park and Walloon Lake; expand his peer group with older, influential reporters; and learn to meet the organizational demands of
the workplace. His assignments gave the cub reporter opportunities to explore his love of action and adventure and took him to the
Fifteenth Street, Number 4 police station and the general hospital.
His boss, Pete Wellington, has said, "He liked action. . . . He always
wanted to be on the scene himself" and recalls that Ernest would
take off in hospital ambulances without letting the city desk know
where he was going or he'd cover crime at the Fifteenth Street station hoping something larger would hit.[27] Eventually, he expanded
his territory and his awareness of the world to Wyoming Street and
covered pool halls and dance halls, where prostitutes did business
and drug sales were rampant, and to the railroad yards, where he
encountered the lives of railroad bums. His experiences fulfilled the
old expression that "Kansas City is a place where boys become men."

Ernest's self-confidence, big smile, and boyish good looks enabled him to make friends easily. He was attracted to older writers such as Lionel Moise, who had a reputation as a "lady's man," was a heavy drinker, and was considered a no-nonsense reporter who admired the works of Mark Twain and Joseph Conrad. Another new friend was Ted Brumback, who had served in France as an ambulance driver before working at the *Star*.

Like many young men of their generation, Ernest and Ted were drawn to the action of the war in Europe. Ernest had written to his sister, Marcelline, "I can't let a show like this go on without getting in on it."[28] Yet, when Ernest turned eighteen and tried to enlist in the army, he was deferred because of poor vision. He had a bad left eye that he probably inherited from his mother, who also had poor vision. However, early in 1918 when Red Cross officials came to Kansas City, Ernest and Brumback quickly signed up to serve as ambulance drivers in Italy. Despite his bad left eye, his dream of getting involved with the war was realized.

Volunteering for the Red Cross not only met Ernest's need for adventure; it had the approval of his parents. Though Dr. Hemingway had not approved of Ernest's serving in the army and was disappointed Ernest had not gone to college, working at the *Kansas City Star* and the decision to serve as a Red Cross volunteer seemed to work. Dr. Hemingway wrote, "I am proud of you and your success" and appreciated the fact that "you have in seven months got a profession that you can take anywhere in the world and earn a living. . . . Both Mother and I love you devotedly."[29] Knowing that Ernest would return to Oak Park before going to Italy, his mother wrote that she was "looking forward to seeing her 'Newspaper Man' home again."[30]

After picking up his final paycheck, Ernest left Kansas City and headed back to Oak Park with plans to return to Michigan for some fishing before leaving for New York and then Italy. As Ernest was about to embark on the adventure he had so longed for, he clearly felt a need to touch base with his roots and those early influences. He went to Oak Park to say good-bye to his family, to Michigan for some fishing, and to his high school to see Miss Biggs. He told her, "If it comes to a death notice for me, I want you to write it, because you'd tell it the way it was, and no gushing."[31]

By May 1918, Ernest was on a train to New York, accompanied by boys from Evanston and New Trier, schools he had played football against in high school. Once in New York, the Red Cross volunteers stayed at the Hotel Earle on Washington Square in Greenwich Village. During his ten-day stay in New York, Ernest made the most of his time and eagerly expanded his world and experiences. He joined newly made friends in visiting the Battery and Grant's Tomb and was invited to parties and dances by New York socialites eager to be hospitable to servicemen.

Mid-May 1918, Ernest boarded the French Line ship *Chicago* in New York for a ten-day passage to Bordeaux and then went on to Paris by train. When Ernest arrived, Paris was being shelled by the Germans, but he didn't let that stop him from continuing to expand his world. With Ted Brumback and his new friend Bill Horne, he visited Napoleon's Tomb, the Hotel des Invalides, the Arc de Triomphe, the Champs-Elysees, and the Tuileries as well as the Follies Bergere. Then on June 6, he boarded a train with other Red Cross volunteers at Gare de Lyon for Milan.

With his arrival in Milan Ernest was initiated into the disasters of war. An explosion in a munitions factory resulted in Red Cross volunteers being rushed to the scene. According to Milford Baker, another volunteer, "The first thing we saw was the body of a woman, legs gone, head gone, intestines strung out. Hemmie and I nearly passed out cold but gritted our teeth and laid the thing on the stretcher." Again, according to Baker, when he and "Hemmie" returned to Milan, they "were the envy of the whole bunch."[32] The grim scene at the munitions plant would later reappear in *Death in the Afternoon* in "The Natural History of the Dead," where he describes the "search [of] the immediate vicinity and surrounding fields for bodies."[33]

In Milan, Hemingway, Baker, Brumback, and Horne were assigned to Section Four, the Red Cross ambulance unit in Schio about four miles from the Austrian line. There Ernest also met John Dos Passos, who was from Chicago and would become a future novelist and lifelong friend. When Ernest's unit chief asked for volunteers to man the canteen stations, Ernest volunteered for a canteen located in a battered farmhouse in an area that had seen much damage in the southeast sector at Fossalta di Piave. He was

Ernest Hemingway seated in a Red Cross ambulance, Italy, 1918. *Hemingway Collection, John F. Kennedy Presidential Library and Museum*

in charge of a relief station behind the lines, where soldiers could get hot food and relax, but also was responsible for bringing chocolate and cigarettes to the Italian soldiers at the front.

Then on July 8, 1918, Ernest was injured by an exploding Austrian mortar shell while passing out American Red Cross canteen supplies to Italian soldiers near Fossalta. According to Bill Horne,

> Ernie grew restless, borrowed a bike and got to the front. He was at an advanced post—a hole in the ground—when the Austrians discovered it and sent over a Minenwerfer. It landed right smack on target. One man was killed, another badly hurt, and Ernie was hit by scaggia [shell fragments]. He dragged out his wounded companion, hoisted him on his back and headed for the trenches a hundred yards away. The Austrians turned their machine guns on him and he took a slug under his knee and another in the ankle but he made it. However, he was stiff legged ever after. No one knew who he was as he lay in the surgical post. Then another ambulance driver came along and identified him.[34]

Ernest's wounds were dressed in Fornaci. Then he was transported to a field hospital in Treviso and after several days to the American Red Cross Hospital in Milan.

The Italian government awarded Ernest with the Medaglia d' Argento al Valore, citing that despite being "gravely wounded by numerous pieces of shrapnel from an enemy shell, with an admirable spirit of brotherhood, before taking care of himself, he rendered generous assistance to the Italian soldiers more seriously wounded by the same explosion and did not allow himself to be carried elsewhere until after they had been evacuated."[35]

Ted Brumback arrived at the Milan hospital as soon as possible and then wrote to Ernest's parents, saying that the concussion of the explosion knocked Ernest unconscious and buried him in earth, that an Italian was instantly killed while another had both his legs blown off. Brumback went on to say that a third Italian was badly wounded and that after Ernest regained consciousness, he put the wounded Italian on his back and carried him to the first aid dugout. Dr. Hemingway wrote back to Ernest, saying, "I do hope and pray you will speedily recover. . . . Dear Mother gets more proud of you every day and hour."[36]

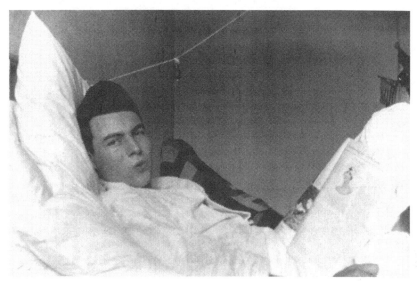

Ernest Hemingway, patient at the American Red Cross Hospital in Milan, 1918. *Ernest Hemingway Foundation of Oak Park*

Later the *Oak Leaves* published a letter that Ernest wrote detailing his wounds and the rescue of the Italian soldier under the headline "Wounded 227 Times," and Dr. Hemingway was requested by members of the First Congregational Church to read aloud from his son's letters. Newsreels played in Chicago theaters showed Ernest in a wheelchair being pushed by a nurse along the hospital terrace. Dressed in his military overcoat, he waved his crutch and smiled. Marcelline, who was the first to see her brother in the theater newsreel, called her parents, and the next evening the whole family went to the theater and shed "tears of joy."

Later Ernest would claim that the depiction of Frederic Henry's wounding in *A Farewell to Arms* came closest to the truth of what he had experienced, writing,

> My legs felt warm and wet and my shoes were wet and warm inside. I knew that I was hit and leaned over and put my hand on my knee. My knee wasn't there. My hand went in and my knee was down on my shin. I wiped my hand on my shirt and another floating light came very slowly down and I looked at my leg and was very afraid. Oh, God, I said, get me out of here.[37]

Though Ernest maintained his positive, energetic nature in the hospital and joked with his family that he would "never look well in kilts," his brush with death had an impact on his outlook on life and the content of his writing.[38] He had encountered death and, at the age of eighteen, had faced danger, endured pain, and behaved with courage. By saving the life of an unknown Italian soldier, he became a hero and the attention he received only increased his self-confidence. He was attractive to women, respected by men, and formally decorated as a hero by the Italian government.

Though he projected a heroic image and maintained his ebullient good nature throughout his recovery, he now understood why death was associated with fear. At first he suffered from insomnia and could not go to sleep without a light on for fear he would die in the night. Eventually, he would use his fear of the dark as a motif in A Farewell to Arms and have his Code Hero Frederic Henry tell the priest, "I am afraid of Him in the night sometimes."[39]

Confrontation of death became one of the most dominant themes in Ernest's novels and the focus of the Code. His characters would be tested by the dangers and horrors of war, and Ernest would use his "own small experiences [as] a touchstone by which [he] could tell whether stories were true or false and being wounded was a password."[40] As Ernest learned to write from his experiences, he used what he learned in Italy to show that war brought out the best and worst in men and women.

Ernest's confrontation with death and his subsequent wound also led to his first experience with love and his encounter with Agnes von Kurowsky, the American nurse he met and fell in love with in the Milan hospital. Agnes had trained as a nurse in New York and upon graduation applied for overseas duty in Italy. She had gray-blue eyes, long chestnut-colored hair, and a comfortable, if not flirtatious, manner with men. Ernest was her first patient in the Red Cross Hospital in Milan. Her diary states that he had "the honor of being the first American wounded in Italy. He has shrapnel in his knees, besides a great many flesh wounds."[41]

After the surgery to repair Ernest's right knee, Agnes would take Ernest outside in a wheelchair, and when he was able to maneuver on crutches, they would have dinners at the Hotel du Nord.

Agnes was nine years older than Ernest and may have just toyed with the emotions of the handsome young American she called a "boy," but when Bill Horne also became a patient at the hospital, he observed Ernest's genuine affection for Agnes.

Throughout his life, Ernest was attracted to women with beautiful hair, and much has been written about the entry in Agnes's diary in which "Mac [another nurse] found one of [Agnes's] yellow hairpins under Hemingway's pillow."[42] Though Agnes later denied any sexual encounters with Ernest, their relationship had a profound impact on him. It is well documented that Agnes was the model for the characterization of Catherine Barkley in A *Farewell to Arms* and likely that Ernest's fascination with her hair inspired the passage where Frederic Henry recalls that he

> loved to take her hair down, . . . take out the pins, lay them on the sheet and it would be loose and I would watch her while she kept very still and then take out the last two pins and it would all come down and she would drop her head and we would both be inside of it, and it was the feeling of inside a tent or behind a falls.[43]

After Ernest's recovery in the Milan hospital, Agnes was transferred to a hospital in Florence, and Ernest briefly was sent back to the front. After the Armistice, Ernest returned to New York and then to Oak Park. When Ernest returned to Oak Park, he believed he and Agnes would someday marry. But with Ernest gone, Agnes was attracted to others. Eventually, she wrote to her "boy" that she planned to marry another. Ernest was heartbroken, or to use his word, "smashed," when she broke up with him. From Oak Park Ernest wrote to Bill Horne, saying, "I've loved Ag. She's been my ideal and Bill I forgot all about religion and everything else—because I had Ag to worship."[44]

Bill Horne met Ernest when he disembarked from the *Guiseppe Verde* on New Year's, 1919. Now Ernest was a hero, and Horne recalled,

> He was a darn dramatic sight. Over six feet tall, wearing a Bersagliere hat with great cock feathers, an enormous officer's cape lined with red satin, a British-style tunic with ribbons of the Valor

Medal and Italian War Cross, and a limp! The *New York Times* carried a front page story and picture, "Most Wound Hero Returns Home Today," while the *Chicago American* noted his return with a headline on page three, "Worst Shot-up Man In US Is On Way Home."[45]

From New York, Ernest took the train to Chicago. Dr. Hemingway and Marcelline met Ernest at the LaSalle Street Station. When they returned to the Kenilworth Avenue house, a collection of neighbors and friends gave Ernest a hero's welcome. Later Frank Platt, one of his high school teachers, asked him to speak to the Debate Club, and at a high school assembly, students memorized a welcoming song, singing, "Hemingway, we hail you the victor / Hemingway, ever winning the game."[46] For months he was in much demand speaking at local clubs and church groups and was the focus of parties hosted by Italian American organizations.

Though Hemingway, the hero and the legend, had been born, the Italian experience not only changed Ernest physically but emotionally. He told his sister Marcelline, "There's a whole big world out there full of people who really feel things . . . sometimes I think we only half live over here."[47] Later he wrote to his friend, Jim Gamble, that he was "homesick for Italy."[48]

Finally, on March 7, 1919, at the home on Kenilworth Avenue in Oak Park, he received the letter he'd been expecting, a devastating letter from Agnes, saying she expected to be married soon but hoped he'd have a wonderful career and "show what a man you really are."[49] Despite, or perhaps because of, being heartbroken, Ernest took her advice. During his "career," he garnered every award valued by a writer, developed a code for living in the twentieth century, and was called "the most fascinating man I know"[50] by one of the world's most beautiful and sexually attractive women.

Chapter Two

─────────○─────────

Demonstrating Awareness of the World beyond Oak Park

For Ernest it must have been something like being put in a box with the cover nailed down to come home to conventional, suburban Oak Park living, after his own vivid experiences.

—Marcelline Hemingway Sanford[1]

Ernest Hemingway outside his boyhood home, 600 N. Kenilworth, Oak Park, Illinois. Having recently returned from Italy, he is wearing his uniform and using a cane due to his leg injuries. *Ernest Hemingway Foundation of Oak Park*

ERNEST HEMINGWAY LEFT THE COMFORT OF HOME and the security of the Midwest and went to Italy looking for adventure. He got more than he had bargained for. The idealistic midwesterner joined the war to end all wars, ready to display honor and courage, but was blown up in a trench. Then he fell in love, contemplated marriage, and was rejected by the woman he loved.

These experiences, along with the people, the culture, and the time spent in Italy, not only changed Ernest's worldview, but helped him to understand and develop it. War revealed itself to the idealistic young ambulance driver not only as a venue for heroism for which one gained medals and recognition, but also as a sordid bloodbath where one was required to carry parts of dead bodies and sustain injuries that would last a lifetime. Ernest learned that modern warfare was different from what Grandfather Anson had experienced, and that being hit by a Minenwerfer was not as heroic as surviving hand-to-hand combat with a sword. As Catherine Barkley would say of her dead boyfriend in A Farewell to Arms, "He didn't have a sabre cut. They blew him all to bits."[2]

The time in Italy, and especially the war experiences, immersed Ernest in a world very different from Oak Park. Surviving in this world required new actions and rituals that trumped some of the religious teachings of his parents and some of the manners and morals learned in Oak Park. In Italy, before he was twenty, he picked up body parts after the munitions factory explosion in Milan. Then he proceeded to the Italian/Austrian front where the soldier next to him was killed, another had his legs blown off, and Ernest was seriously injured. These experiences forged a philosophy of life that didn't exist and wasn't needed in Oak Park.

In this new world where God didn't intervene and the old rules didn't seem to matter, Ernest began to formulate a new model for moral conduct. As these actions and rituals evolved, they became the basis for the Hemingway Code and the set of morals and rules needed for survival in the modern world. Using this Code, Ernest created modern heroes and a code of conduct for a world where heroes faced death without the comfort of religion or engaging in self-pity. Through their actions, these heroes would exhibit "grace under pressure."

Despite or because of these life-changing experiences, Ernest returned to Oak Park with a zest for life and a motivation to try new things that would endure for the rest of his life. After his experiences in Italy, Oak Park wasn't really home anymore. As a result, he was free to explore new places and expand his interests with new friends. As it would turn out, he would have a lifelong interest in wars, and they would become the settings for his modern heroes to demonstrate grace under pressure and live by the new moral code.

When Ernest returned from Italy to Oak Park, his self-confidence was strong and the handsome young man still in uniform enjoyed a hero's welcome. Neighbors stopped by the house to see him, his teachers invited him back to the high school to share his experiences with their students, and the Chicago Italian-American clubs hosted several elaborate parties in his honor. Despite the notoriety, however, there was sadness. Most of his high school friends were away at college, and he wasn't able to get a job because the pain in his leg kept him from standing more than a few hours at a time. Most of his spare time was filled with reading. Like Krebs in "Soldier's Home," he confronted a family life that he no longer felt a part of and a set of goals and values he could only partially embrace.

When summer came, the family went to Michigan as usual, but Ernest slept late and didn't do much writing. He spent the fall in nearby Petoskey. As a result of a talk he gave to the Ladies' Aid Society at the Petoskey Library, he met Mrs. Harriet Connable and was invited to spend the winter in Toronto to be the companion to her disabled son, Ralph Connable Jr., who was one year younger than Ernest. During that winter, Mr. Connable, who was head of F. W. Woolworth in Canada, introduced Ernest to his friends at the *Toronto Star*. This crucial introduction led to opportunities for Ernest to write occasional articles for the *Star* until he returned to Oak Park in May 1920.

The summer of 1920 was difficult. Dr. Hemingway did not go to Michigan but stayed in Oak Park to work and hopefully bolster family finances. Ernest was supposed to take care of Dr. Hemingway's usual Michigan chores but didn't fulfill his duties or live up to his family's work ethic. Following his twenty-first birthday, his mother told him he either had to move out or get a job. According to his sister Marcelline, Ernest "resented" the ultimatum but moved to Chicago and got a job as an editorial assistant on the staff of *Cooperative Commonwealth*.[3] He lived with Kenley Smith and his wife, Doodles, and it was through them he met Hadley Elizabeth Richardson.

Hadley and Ernest seemed to look to one another to define their lives and their futures. Ernest had chosen not to go to college but rather to pursue writing. Hadley had dropped out of Bryn Mawr College and devoted herself to playing the piano. Ernest was no longer comfortable living with his parents, and Hadley was without a home. Her father committed suicide when she was twelve, and her mother had just died of Bright's disease after a long and painful illness. Though she was twenty-nine years old and Ernest was barely twenty-one, he was attracted to her athletic good looks and her beautiful auburn hair.

By the fall of 1921, Ernest appeared to have readjusted to his family's midwestern values. He had a job and a future wife of whom his family approved and had even published his first poems. On September 3, 1921, Ernest and Hadley were married at the First Presbyterian Church in Horton Bay, Michigan, and at the family's invitation, they spent their honeymoon at the cottage on Walloon Lake. Thirty guests attended their wedding in the little church decorated with Michigan wildflowers. After a wedding dinner, Ernest rowed his wife across the lake to the family cottage, where they slept on the floor in front of the fireplace on a mattress pulled from one of the beds.

Soon Mr. and Mrs. Ernest Hemingway were guests of honor at Clarence and Grace's twenty-fifth wedding anniversary party, and more good news came when the Italian Consulate in Chicago informed Ernest that General Diaz was coming to Chicago to present him with the Croce di Guerra Medal and a pension of fifty lira per year for life.

After Ernest and Hadley had settled in an apartment at 1239 North Dearborn Parkway in Chicago, Ernest received an offer to be a foreign correspondent for the *Toronto Star*, and the couple jumped at the opportunity to move to Paris. Sherwood Anderson, who had convinced Ernest that Paris was a good place for a young writer, gave him letters of introduction to Gertrude Stein and Ezra Pound among others. In addition to Ernest's having a real job, Hadley now received trust funds from her mother's estate, so with income and letters of introduction, the stage for a new life in Paris was set. They sailed on the French liner *Leopoldina* on December 8, 1921.

With limited income but much enthusiasm, Ernest and Hadley moved into an apartment at 74 rue du Cardinal Lemoine in

Ernest Hemingway and Hadley Richardson on their wedding day, Horton Bay, Michigan, September 3, 1921. They spent their honeymoon across the lake at the family's cottage. *Ernest Hemingway Foundation of Oak Park*

Ernest and Hadley Hemingway's first apartment at 1239 N. Dearborn Parkway, Chicago. *N. Sindelar Collection*

the Latin Quarter on the Left Bank near the Place de la Contres-carpe on December 22, 1921. The fourth-floor walk-up was in a working-class neighborhood and above an all-night dance hall or *bal musette*. It contained only two rooms: a living room, where Hadley kept her rented piano, and a bedroom. The kitchen, which was a small attachment to the living room, had a two-burner gas stove. The bathroom consisted of a Turkish toilet located at the bend of the stairs and a bowl, water pitcher, and slop jar located in the bedroom closet. The only heat came from the living room fireplace, and any garbage had to be carried down four steep flights of circular stairs. Neither Ernest nor Hadley had grown up in these kinds of conditions. Yet, the rent at 250 francs a month, about $18, fit their budget, and Ernest wrote to his parents that the apartment was "the jolliest place you ever saw."[4]

With Hadley's trust income of $3,000 a year, Ernest's war pension, and yearly earnings of $1,500 from the *Toronto Star* and a good exchange rate of U.S. dollars to French francs, Ernest and Hadley explored French restaurants, drank good wine, and partici-pated in a lifestyle that was new and exhilarating to both of them. Hadley spent long hours practicing the piano, and Ernest wrote in the open-air cafés and observed with great interest fellow expatri-ates and writers.

The combination of Ernest's intense curiosity, good looks, and self-confidence allowed him to make friends easily. Soon he was part of a circle of American writers that included John Dos Passos and Archibald MacLeish, and he quickly used his letters of introduction from Sherwood Anderson to meet Gertrude Stein and Ezra Pound.

When Ernest and Hadley first arrived in Paris, Ernest was writing articles for the *Toronto Star* as well as working on his own poetry and short stories. At this point his identity as a writer was not clear, to neither Ernest nor anyone else. Was he a poet, a short story writer, or a journalist? He worked feverishly at all three genres and was emotionally and financially supported by Hadley, who had total confidence in Ernest as a writer.

Ezra Pound, quick to recognize Hemingway's talent as a poet, submitted six of Hemingway's poems to the *Dial*, for which he was a talent scout. The poems were rejected but later published at the recommendation of Pound in *Poetry* magazine in Chicago. Pound also expanded Ernest's literary education by introducing him to

Ernest and Hadley's Paris apartment at 74 rue Cardinal Lemoine. *N. Sindelar Collection*

Closerie de Lilas, a quiet café on Boulevard du Montparnasse, where Ernest wrote and met with friends Scott Fitzgerald and John Dos Passos. *N. Sindelar Collection*

James Joyce and T. S. Eliot. Their works, as well as the work of other modernists, were easily accessed in Sylvia Beach's lending library at Shakespeare and Company, which Ernest visited frequently.

The Pound protégés, Joyce and Eliot, provided Ernest with new examples of style: let action speak for itself, don't tell readers how to respond, eliminate superfluous words, fear abstractions, and use symbols that arise naturally from the story. Years later Ernest would summarize what he learned from his Paris mentors in *A Movable Feast*, saying, "If I started to write elaborately . . . I found that I could cut that scrollwork or ornament out and throw it away and start with the first true simple declarative sentence I had written . . . it was good and severe discipline."[5]

When he was not writing poetry, he reflected on his boyhood experiences in Michigan and worked on short stories. Using the advice gained from Pound, he developed a style of prose that was declarative, void of abstractions, and free from unnecessary adjectives and adverbs. Eventually, Pound would introduce Ernest to Robert McAlmon, who would publish three hundred copies of *Three Stories and Ten Poems* in 1923. The Michigan stories, "Up in Michigan," "Out of Season," and "My Old Man," would be the basis for this publication.

Though frustrated by numerous rejection letters he received from publishers refusing to publish his poetry and short stories, Ernest was successful at portraying life in Europe to the readers of the *Toronto Star*. Because the *Toronto Star* received information about world events from various news services, Ernest was free to write about whatever he wished. His experience at the *Kansas City Star* made him a careful observer and reporter of events, while his innate interest in action drew him to situations that were of great interest to Toronto readers. Whether it was politics in France or sledding in Switzerland, Ernest wrote articles that were told with authority and filled with action.

Having been in France less than two weeks and only able to speak a few words of French, he already understood the intensity of conversation and opinion exchanged in the cafés of Paris. He wrote with certainty about his café observations of French politics and the political future of Georges Clemenceau, saying,

> In the cafes the Frenchmen have nothing to gain or lose by the things they say, so they consequently say the things they believe. . . . And if you catch enough Frenchmen in different parts of the France, you will have the national opinion; the real national opinion, not the shadow of the national opinion that is reflected in elections and newspapers.[6]

His conclusion, based on French café opinion, was that Clemenceau "lived too long after his job was finished, and now, as the Frenchman in the café said, 'he must wait until he is dead to be a great man again.'"[7]

Using his background in journalism and his keen skills of observation, he also nurtured the craft of catching the intensity of action and the details of the place and the people in articles sent back to his readers in Canada. To escape the dampness of Paris, Ernest and Hadley would retreat to Chamby-sur-Montreux in Switzerland for sledding and skiing. They stayed in a simple mountain chalet in Chamby, a thousand feet above Lake Geneva (Lac Leman), and skied and rode bobsleds at Les Avants. There he captured the excitement of bobsledding, saying to his Toronto readers, "If you want a thrill of the sort that starts at the base of your spine in a shiver and ends with you nearly swallowing your heart . . . try bobsledding on a mountain road at 50 miles an hour."[8]

Eventually, Ernest would say to Max Perkins that "whatever success I have had has been through writing what I know about."[9] Years later Ernest also would recall his Swiss mountain experiences and the warm comfort of a Swiss feather bed, saying in *A Farewell to Arms*, "When I undressed I opened the windows and saw the night and the cold stars and the pine trees below the window and then got into bed as fast as I could. It was lovely in bed with the air so cold and clear."[10]

Though Oak Park was no longer home, many of the Oak Park values remained. His study of classical literature and his lifelong interest in reading, nurtured by his parents and expanded during

Ernest Hemingway sledding at Les Avants near Montreux, Switzerland. *Hemingway Collection, John F. Kennedy Presidential Library and Museum*

his high school years, enabled him to absorb both the old and new literary ideas and conventions he encountered in France and Switzerland. Not far from Montreux was the Castle of Chillon. Down in the dungeon among the graffiti, Ernest and Hadley discovered the name Byron carved into the pillar where Bonivad, the prisoner immortalized in the poem "Prison of Chillon," once was chained. Given his background in English literature, it's likely that Ernest would have remembered that Byron and Shelley stopped to visit the Château de Chillon while visiting the area around Lake Geneva (Lac Leman), and that the poem was inspired by Byron's experiences as a visitor to the Continent.

Similarly, Ernest's love of reading also drew him to Shakespeare and Company. Sylvia Beach's Paris bookstore supported new writers and stocked English-language books. Her lending library contained the works of Joyce, Eliot, and Pound as well as racks of English and American periodicals and helped to expand Ernest's literary world and influence the content and style of his writing.

Most notable of all, however, was his commitment to the midwestern work ethic and his intense desire to define himself as a writer. He traveled to any event that would create an interesting article for the *Star*. When the Greco-Turkish War broke out, he was there. Against Hadley's wishes he left Paris and spent four days and three nights on the Orient Express to Constantinople. When the armistice was signed in the fall of 1922, he wrote vivid reports on the Greek exodus from Thrace, observing the retreating peasants while walking miles across the Maritza Valley toward Macedonia. He followed the "silent, ghastly procession" of displaced humanity and observed the "exhausted, staggering men, women and children, blankets over their heads, walking blindly along in the rain beside their worldly goods."[11] When he returned to Paris from the Greco-Turkish War in fall 1922, he was taking quinine to reduce his fever and his head was shaved as a result of sleeping in lice-infected beds.

In 1922 he was dispatched to cover the Greco-Turkish Peace Conference held at the Chateau Ouchy in Lausanne. There he observed the action and opinions of Benito Mussolini, and his lifelong interest in debunking intellectualism and arrogant politicians was born. Using his skills of observation, he brought Mussolini's

Ernest Hemingway and Robert McAlmon outside a bullring in Spain, 1923.
Hemingway Collection, John F. Kennedy Presidential Library and Museum

political opinions to life by focusing on the man's personal characteristics, clothes, and intellectual pretensions. Though Ernest's
dislike of Fascist governments would only continue to grow, he was
quick to call Mussolini "the biggest bluff in Europe."[12] This opinion
was based in part on seeing Mussolini studying a book in front of
a group of reporters. Rather than being impressed with this apparent façade of intellectualism, Ernest crept behind Mussolini and
discovered he was actually "studying" a French-English dictionary
and that he was holding it upside down. His article for the *Toronto
Star* said that Mussolini clothed "small ideas in big words,"[13] and
that "there is something wrong, even histrionically, with a man who
wears white spats with a black shirt."[14]

When he wasn't writing articles for the *Star*, Ernest spent hours
at the cafés along Boulevard du Montparnasse, working on his poetry and short stories. Though he was becoming a fixture in Paris,
he did not identify with the American expatriate artist crowd that
frequented La Rotonde. He thought they were lazy and phony and
wrote a scathing indictment of this group for the *Toronto Star*.

> You can find anything you are looking for at the Rotonde—except
> serious artists . . . for the artists of Paris who are turning out cred-
> itable work resent and loathe the Rotonde crowd. . . . They are
> nearly all loafers . . . talking about what they are going to do and
> condemning the work of all artists who have gained any degree
> of recognition.[15]

Despite his disdain for those who posed as artists, Ernest
quickly made friends and sought out literary influences that were
helpful to his writing and career. Though he and Hadley had
planned to return to Chamby-sur-Montreux for the winter of 1923,
they quickly left Chamby when Ezra Pound encouraged them to
visit him in Rapallo, Italy. Despite their careful planning, however,
there were other surprises that winter too. Convinced Ernest would
want to work on his fiction and poetry while in Switzerland, Hadley
packed all of Ernest's literary papers and then lost them on the train
trip to Chamby. Though Ernest did not blame her for the loss, she
was devastated, her emotions no doubt being enhanced by the fact
that she now was pregnant.

As it turned out, Pound spent much of his time at the Vatican Library researching his *Cantos*. Yet, the three days Ernest spent with Pound in Rapallo were filled with thoughtful discussions about the importance of accuracy of historical facts and geography in fiction. It was in Rapallo too that Ernest met Robert McAlmon, who had a broad range of literary connections in New York and Paris. Pound's absence accelerated Ernest's friendship with McAlmon, who ultimately published *Three Stories and Ten Poems* and introduced Ernest to Spain and bullfighting.

In June 1923, Ernest and Robert McAlmon met Bill Bird in Madrid and then traveled to Seville, Ronda, Granada, and back to Madrid while Hadley stayed in Paris in her sixth month of pregnancy. Ernest was captivated by the bullfights. They engaged the man who as a child told his mother he was "'fraid of nothing" and dramatized a code of behavior that endorsed physical endurance and courage. Ernest saw immediately that a good matador personified "grace under pressure" and that the bullring was a place where risk taking and coping with death could be studied. The trip expanded Ernest's knowledge of the world and developed his concept of the Code. He vowed he would return to Spain for the Festival of San Fermin in Pamplona.

Despite his newfound fascination with Spain, however, Ernest was about to become a father. He and Hadley decided that the baby should be born in Toronto and that Ernest would return as a full-time reporter for the *Toronto Star*. After much work on his writing and many new European experiences, Ernest Hemingway, the war hero, veteran reporter, and experienced European traveler, would now return to a regular job and begin life as a parent. His reluctance regarding the return to a more traditional lifestyle can be seen in the fact that he did not tell his parents about the baby until three weeks before Hadley delivered. Also, Clarence and Grace Hemingway did not see their grandson until 1927 when Hadley brought the boy to Oak Park.

Everyone worked to make the transition to life in Toronto a positive experience. Ernest's parents were overjoyed at the news of Hadley's pregnancy, and some of Ernest's Oak Park belongings and Hadley's St. Louis furniture were shipped to the fourth-floor

Ernest and Hadley's Toronto apartment at 1599 Bathurst Street. *Brian Gordon Sinclair Collection*

walk-up apartment at 1599 Bathurst Street. Though a small apartment, it was comfortable and had a sunroom. Ernest wrote to Marcelline, "We have a very lovely place here just on the edge of the country across a ravine from the Hunt Club. It is very beautiful, new, light, airy, beautifully and tastefully furnished by ourselves, full of electric fixtures and bath tubs."[16] He added, however, "We hope not to have to stay here long as we are both homesick for Paris where there are few bath tubs, no electric fixtures, but very nearly all the charm, all the good food and most of the good people in the world."[17]

Once back in Toronto, Ernest was required to work long hours on assignments he thought were inconsequential and had little time to work on writing of his own. The *Toronto Star* sent him to places that were dull in comparison to his European assignments, and he resented the fact that he was returning from Montreal by train and ten miles outside of Toronto when his son was born on October 10, 1923. When he was asked to write a story about the white peacock the *Star* had purchased for the Toronto Zoo, he had had enough, and he and Hadley decided to return to Paris.

Ernest made an obligatory trip to Oak Park for Christmas; then he, Hadley, and John (Bumby) headed back to Paris in January 1924. Despite numerous gifts for the baby and his parents' payment of the hospital bill, Ernest's separation from Oak Park continued to widen. That Christmas he gave his sister Marcelline a copy of *Three Stories and Ten Poems*, but told her not to show it to their parents, thinking they would be offended by the content. He did not return to Oak Park until the 1928 death of his father.

The return to Paris defined Ernest as a writer, not a journalist. His ties with the *Toronto Star* were severed, and his only source of income was Hadley's trust fund and whatever funds he received for reviewing manuscripts for Ford Madox Ford's *Transatlantic Review*. The decision to focus on writing was reflected in the location of their new apartment at 113 rue Notre-Dame-des-Champs. The apartment was in the Montparnasse neighborhood, the center of intellectual and artistic life of Paris. It was close to Ezra Pound's studio at 70 bis rue Notre-Dame-des-Champs, Sylvia Beach's bookstore, and Gertrude Stein's apartment on the rue de Fleurus.

Ernest and Hadley's Paris apartment at 113 rue Notre-Dame-des-Champs. *Hemingway Collection, John F. Kennedy Presidential Library and Museum.*

John N. Hemingway (Bumby) with one of his godparents, Gertrude Stein, in the Luxembourg Gardens, Paris. *Hemingway Collection, John F. Kennedy Presidential Library and Museum*

Nearby were the Luxembourg Gardens, where they could stroll with Bumby, and the Closerie des Lilas, a quiet café on the Boulevard du Montparnasse that Ernest liked because few, if any, of the expatriate crowd spent time there.

Though the rent at 650 francs a month, about $30, was more than the Cardinal Lemoine rent, their apartment had a small kitchen, dining room, bedroom, and sitting room with a stove. While the new apartment had more space, there was no electricity and no toilet and it was above a lumberyard. The buzz of saws was constant from 7 a.m. to 5 p.m. The baby slept in the dining room, and his borrowed buggy was kept in the lumberyard.

Once again Ernest worked feverishly on his writing. Back again in Paris he found his voice. He wrote stories about his boyhood in Michigan in lean, economical prose, but he was confronted as well as conflicted by the moral restraints of middle-class America. When the American Women's Club of Paris canceled their subscription to the *Transatlantic Review*, he understood their objections. When the New York publisher Boni and Liveright demanded the replacement of "Up in Michigan" for fear of censorship problems with *In Our Time*, Ernest had to weigh his desire to be published against his desire to honestly portray the sexuality of a male-female relationship.

Ernest was well versed in the moral code of Prohibition-era America. It was similar to the moral education he had received from his parents. His father believed social dancing, card playing, and gambling were wrong and forbade smoking and drinking alcoholic beverages. Though it was good to bring children into the world, sexual activity was not a topic for discussion.

His family's values were consistent and clear. Christian religious principles, a traditional education, and a strong work ethic were imparted to Ernest as a child and nurtured via frequent letters after he left Oak Park. As a child, he always was expected to be doing something useful. Dr. Hemingway had no patience for just sitting around or relaxing in a chair and had little room for compromise between what he considered right and wrong. If his children were wrong, they were either sent to their rooms without supper or spanked with a razor strop. After the punishment, they were to kneel down and ask God for forgiveness.

In his early life, Ernest benefited from the discipline and the education as well as the warmth and acceptance his parents provided. Family values were reinforced by the frequent interaction with both parents, who raised active, well-read, self-confident children. Ernest learned to hunt and fish with his father, and his mother complemented the family values with warmth and affection. Both parents set clear limits, but encouraged Ernest to grow "every day in strength of character and purpose to make your life count for the best things."[18]

As a young adult, however, he seemed to believe that this condition of comfort and support would be challenged by his efforts to write clearly and honestly about life in the modern world. Because of his experiences in Europe, he had developed an autonomous morality, in which his personal standards were different from those of his parents. He knew it and tried to bridge the gap with explanatory letters home. Writing to his father from Paris, he said,

> You see I'm trying in all my stories to get the feeling of actual life—not to just depict life—or criticize it—but to actually make it alive. So that when you have read something by me you actually experience the thing. You can't do this without putting the bad and the ugly as well as what is beautiful. Because if it is all beautiful you can't believe in it. Things aren't that way. It is only by showing both sides—3 dimensions and if possible 4 that you can write the way I want to.
>
> So when you see anything of mine that you don't like remember that I'm sincere in doing it and that I'm working toward something. If I write an ugly story that might be hateful to you or to Mother the next one might be one that you would like exceedingly.[19]

In Our Time was a pivotal piece in Ernest's writing and commitment to a new set of values. His letter to his father about the ugly as well as the beautiful, no doubt, was to prepare him for this transition. In Our Time, a collection of stories interspersed with the previously written vignettes also called in our time, asks and answers questions that no doubt concerned the author. What is a man? What is bravery? What is fear? What constitutes a good relationship between a man and a woman? Answers to these questions were based on a new set of values and described with honesty and images that were sometimes blunt, sexual, or bloody.

He explored subjects considered taboo in Oak Park. He began to question values such as marriage, saying in "The Three-Day Blow," "Once a man's married he's absolutely bitched. . . . They get this sort of fat married look. They're done for."[20] Sexual relationships and their consequences also were examined. In "Up in Michigan," Ernest details the seduction of Liz Coates, who begins by protesting, "You mustn't do it, Jim. You mustn't . . . Oh, it isn't right" and ends with "Oh, Jim, Jim. Oh."[21]

Growing up in Oak Park with an obstetrician father, Ernest was fully aware of the painful and bloody birthing process. His father was chief of obstetrics at Oak Park Hospital and had a medical office in the family home. His mother continued to have children until she was forty-three and Ernest was fifteen. When Ernest was eleven, he was present at the birth of his sister Carol at the family cottage in Michigan. Now in "Indian Camp" he would detail the birthing process with Nick's father, Dr. Adams, performing a Cesarean section with a jackknife.

These early stories as well as the later novels contained many autobiographical, and sometimes unflattering, clues pointing to Ernest's parents and friends. The doctor in "The Doctor and the Doctor's Wife" is reminiscent of Dr. Hemingway in that he hires local Indians to do chores and has a gun he's very fond of and a wife who takes to her darkened bedroom with headaches. Though the doctor is portrayed as weak in not standing up to the Indians in a conflict over a stolen log and the wife is pious and unsympathetic to her husband, Dr. Hemingway appeared to overlook the negative, family-based characterizations and continued to support Ernest's writing by saying he had a good memory for details and wishing he'd send his work more often.

Though Ernest yearned for the continued support of his family, his changing values were well nourished by his friends and neighbors on the Left Bank, if not totally supported or understood by his family. Gertrude Stein called the Left Bank people the "lost generation," knowing that this group no longer embraced the values of their elders, the advice of their fathers, or the sayings of their mothers, but were forging their way through a new world. They were "lost" because they truly weren't at home in either world. The old, pre–World War I values no longer worked, and a new set of values or rules by which to live had yet to be clearly defined.

Despite being "lost," there was, however, much experimentation with a new way of living. Sex was an open topic for conversation, and homosexual and bisexual relationships were common. Robert McAlmon, who published Ernest's first book and introduced him to Spain, was sexually ambiguous and attracted to both men and women. He was married to an English heiress, who supported his writing and publishing efforts, but enjoyed bisexual relationships and wrote stories about transvestite drag queens and male homosexuals.

Gertrude Stein partnered with Alice B. Toklas, and the two Jewish lesbians became the godparents of Ernest and Hadley's son, John (Bumby). Ernest enjoyed visiting their large studio filled with Cézannes, Matisses, and Picassos. There he drank natural distilled liqueurs made from fruits and accepted Gertrude's counsel regarding his writing and her encouragement to collect art.

After Bumby was baptized in his father's baptismal gown at the Episcopal chapel of St. Luke's in the Garden in May 1924, Ernest combined the old values with the new by writing to his parents, saying, "Don't worry about JHN's spiritual welfare. . . . He is a member in good standing of the Church of England and has both god mothers and god fathers who are sworn to instruct him in religious things as he grows up. He will probably be found occupying a much higher place in the heavenly grandstand than any of his Congregational relatives."[22]

By summer 1924, Bumby was weaned, and Ernest and Hadley left Bumby in Paris with their *femme de manage* and went to the Festival of San Fermin in Pamplona. Ernest's hunger for the bullfights was fueled by his fascination with action, ritual, and death. The action came from the bravery and precise work of the matadors, the ritual from the defined stages of the bullfight; and the death of the bull was the result of the matador's ability to show grace under pressure while slipping the sword into the exact spot between the bull's shoulders—a clear, precise death when done correctly. To these events Ernest brought his early training as a marksman, his reporter's eye for detail, and his curiosity about how one faces death. He now knew there was no chance to face a mortar shell bravely and that no courage was required of a passive victim. Yet in the bullring the early lessons about honor and courage from Grandfather Anson seemed to be relevant, and he studied the matador's moves closely.

Returning to Paris from Spain, Ernest was both charged by the physical, emotional, and intellectual qualities of the bullfight and pleased with what he had accomplished after leaving Toronto. He had written ten new stories and all but finished *In Our Time*. He continued to work on his writing and the selection and editing of fiction for the *Transatlantic Review* and broadened his circle of friends to include Scott and Zelda Fitzgerald, Gerald and Sara Murphy, and Pauline Pfeiffer. The winter of 1924–1925 was spent skiing in Schruns, Austria, and another trip to Spain was planned for July 1925.

The 1925 trip to Pamplona included friends and acquaintances that populated the cafés on Boulevard du Montparnasse and later became the basis for characters in the *The Sun Also Rises*. In the novel, a group of Paris expatriates attend the fiesta. The friends are members of the lost generation, and their days at the fiesta are filled with mindless drinking, squabbles, and dissipation. Though the book was originally entitled *Lost Generation* and then *Fiesta*, Ernest eventually linked this lost generation to biblical verses from Ecclesiastes: "One generation passeth away, and another generation cometh; but the earth abideth for ever. The sun also ariseth, and the sun goeth down, and hasteth to the place where he arose."[23]

The success of the novel came in part from the careful merging of the old values with some of the new. In the midst of the heavy drinking and meaningless revelry of the lost generation characters, Pedro Romero, the matador, becomes a hero because he conducts himself with honor and courage. He stands out in contrast to the expat crowd, who have "lost touch with the soil." As Bill Groton says to Jake Barnes, the impotent war correspondent, "You get precious. Fake European standards have ruined you. You drink yourself to death. You become obsessed by sex.

Ernest and Hadley Hemingway in Pamplona, Spain, with Pauline Pfeiffer and others, 1925. *Hemingway Collection, John F. Kennedy Presidential Library and Museum*

You spend all you time talking, not working. You are an expatriate, see? You hang around cafes."[24]

Though *The Sun Also Rises* was well received by the critics, it was not well received by Ernest's friends who saw themselves portrayed as self-indulgent, alcoholic, and sexually promiscuous in his unflattering, but honest, characterizations. Nor was it well received by his parents. Grace wrote that he had produced "one of the filthiest books of the year,"[25] while his father said, "You surely are now famous as a writer and I shall trust your future books will have a different sort of subject matter. You have such wonderful ability and we want to be able to read and ask others to enjoy your works."[26]

Despite the mixed reviews from critics, friends, and family, Ernest sensed the potential success of *The Sun Also Rises* and worked to break his contract with Boni and Liveright by writing *The Torrents of Spring*. In doing so, he satirized the work of Sherwood Anderson, a popular Boni and Liveright author, so that Boni and Liveright would refuse to publish *Torrents*, and he would then be free to send the manuscript of *The Sun Also Rises* to Max Perkins at Scribner's. While Hadley did not support Ernest's use of their longtime friend Sherwood Anderson to further his publication interests, Pauline Pfeiffer did.

Pauline was part of a growing circle of friends who were rich, influential, and potentially helpful to Ernest's career. She had joined Ernest and Hadley in Pamplona and then went to Schruns for Christmas and New Year's 1926 before returning to Paris. During the winter of 1926 while Hadley was in Schruns, Austria, Ernest went to New York to terminate his contract with Boni and Liveright and pursue a new relationship with Scribner's. When he returned to Paris, he met with Pauline.

By the end of 1926, he had broken with his publisher, Boni and Liveright; distanced himself from his loyal friend Sherwood Anderson; and separated from Hadley and Bumby. While his career was advancing, so were his tendencies to pursue a life of physical and emotional risk taking and danger. During the Paris years he had reaped rewards for leaving his Midwest home and branching out to meet new people and see new places. Now, again, he was feeding that hunger, if not addiction, for the intensity and freedom that came from leaving "home," wherever that home or place might be.

Chapter Three

---◯---

The Key West Attraction

Afraid of nothing.

—Ernest Hemingway to his mother, 1901[1]

Ernest Hemingway with a lion on his 1933–1934 African safari. *Hemingway Collection, John F. Kennedy Presidential Library and Museum*

WHEN ERNEST WAS ONLY A TODDLER, he told his mother that he was "'fraid of nothing,"[2] that "when I get to be a big boy . . . I want to go with Dad and shoot lions and wolves."[3] As time passed his tenacity was cultivated by his father and his grandfathers as well as the companions Ernest chose to befriend throughout his life.

His father taught him the skills necessary to meet and enjoy the challenges of hunting and fishing. Clarence Hemingway told his children that "accidents don't happen to people who know how to handle guns. . . . Treat a gun like a friend. Keep it clean. Oil it, clean it after every use, but always remember, it's an enemy if it's carelessly used."[4] He also took his children into deep water, deliberately rocked the boat until it capsized, and told his children to "swim for shore!"[5] Ernest and his siblings found their father's lifesaving drills exciting and were keen about the competitive swimming races to shore. At a young age, they learned to exercise "grace under pressure."

Ernest's grandfathers nurtured his lifelong fascination of war with frequent displays of guns and medals as well as stories of courage and honor and later letters of encouragement sent to the Italian front. Ernest's letters to his family from Italy reflect his pride in his military conduct, his courageous behavior under fire, and his stoic good humor while in the hospital. Like his early role models, Ernest grew to value physical endurance and courage, values that influenced his lifelong interest in hunting and fishing, his participation in high school athletics and boxing, and his fascination with the manifestations of physical endurance and courage that surfaced in war as well as in the bullring.

"Grace under pressure" was a behavior studied by Ernest throughout his life, and it was demonstrated by his heroes, regardless of whether they were facing a wartime enemy, a charging bull, or a great marlin. The phrase first was defined by Ernest while skiing in Schruns, Austria, with Gerald Murphy and John Dos Passos. Skiing through trees toward the base of the mountain required the men to not only negotiate the snow and the pitch of the terrain but also navigate through the trees. Despite the fact that Ernest stopped often to check on their well-being, Gerald Murphy and John Dos Passos were terrified by the experience. Ernest, however, found the adventure exhilarating and told his friends "he knew what courage was. It was grace under pressure." He felt "absolutely elated."[6]

While it's well documented that Ernest tested his physical endurance and courage by skiing through trees, hunting big game in Africa, and even facing bulls in the ring, his risk-taking behavior also impacted his personal relationships. During the Kansas City days, he admired Lionel Moise, a forceful veteran journalist who wrote argumentative stories with confidence. During the Paris years, he took literary risks by developing characters encountered on the streets. Writing about homosexuals, dope fiends, and prostitutes caused him to be challenged by critics and friends who called his work vulgar or sordid. At one point, he complained to Fitzgerald that "friends" would send him any reviews that said his books were "a pile of shit."[7] Then despite the advice of Hadley, he published *The Torrents of Spring*, which chastised his loyal friend and supporter Sherwood Anderson, in order to break his contract with Boni and Liveright. As time passed, he not only sought adventures that challenged his physical safety, but also his emotional safety.

Perhaps his biggest emotional challenge was his relationship with Pauline Pfeiffer. When he met Pauline, he still loved Hadley. Hadley supported his writing emotionally and financially and

Ernest Hemingway skiing in Schruns, Austria, with Gerald Murphy and John Dos Passos, 1926. *Hemingway Collection, John F. Kennedy Presidential Library and Museum*

Ernest and Pauline Pfeiffer Hemingway, Paris, 1927. *Hemingway Collection, John F. Kennedy Presidential Library and Museum*

Ernest and Pauline Hemingway's apartment at 6 rue Ferou, Paris. *N. Sindelar Collection*

enthusiastically participated in Ernest's skiing, fishing, and bullfighting expeditions. She also was the mother of his son, whom he
also loved and felt responsible for. Yet, as the Toronto experience
proved, Ernest did not do well with routine. He thrived on excitement and emotional highs and could not withdraw from his affair
with Pauline. Hadley recognized the attraction and gave Ernest a
choice. She said if he and Pauline would separate for one hundred
days and then still wanted to be together after the separation, she
would consent to a divorce. In less than one hundred days, however, Hadley recognized her marriage to Ernest was over, filed for
divorce, and moved with Bumby to an apartment at 35 rue des
Fleurus near Gertrude Stein and Alice B. Toklas's salon.

On May 10, 1927, Ernest and Pauline were married in a
Catholic ceremony at L'Eglise de St.Honore-d Eylau on the place
Victor Hugo. Then Ernest and Pauline moved to an antique-filled
apartment at 6 rue Ferou near the Luxembourg Gardens. Pauline
had selected an apartment that had a salon, dining room, full
kitchen, large bedroom, and a study, where Ernest could write.
While Pauline was younger, thinner, and more stylish than Hadley, she too was utterly devoted to Ernest Hemingway the writer.
Early in their friendship, she would visit Hadley and Ernest to
hear the latest chapter of *Torrents* and was, in fact, one of the
few people who supported its publication. Later she typed his
manuscripts and provided a lifestyle that nurtured his career as a
writer. A graduate of the University of Missouri's School of Journalism, Pauline first worked on the night desk at the *Cleveland
Star*. Then her career path took her to New York and *Vanity Fair*,
whose publisher then reassigned her to Paris, where she covered
fashion shows for *Vogue*.

Like Hadley, Pauline came from St. Louis, but her family was
more successful financially, and her trust fund was larger than
Hadley's. Her father had developed a chain of drugstores in Missouri and then purchased sixty thousand acres of lucrative Arkan-
sas farmland, while her adoring uncle Gus held controlling stock
in Warner Pharmaceuticals and Richard Hudnut Cosmetics. Her
mother raised Pauline as a devout Catholic and sent Pauline and
her sister to Catholic girls' schools before they went on to college.

Though it was popular and very French to have a wife at home and a mistress on the side, this type of arrangement wasn't going to work for Ernest and Pauline. Marriage within the Catholic Church was required. As a result, Ernest used the "extreme unction" given to him after he was injured in Italy as the basis for declaring that he was a Catholic. Though he never embraced the strict Protestantism of his parents, his conversion to Catholicism does seem rather convenient. Since Hadley was not Catholic, the conversion annulled his marriage to her and allowed his marriage to Pauline.

Despite the convenient timing of his religious conversion, there is evidence that Ernest was interested in Catholicism even before he met Pauline. His articles for the *Toronto Star* and his characterizations of the "lost generation" in *The Sun Also Rises* reveal he was troubled by the dissipation of the post–World War I world and was searching for values and meaning in what seemed to be a godless world.

Letters to his friends also reveal his interest in Catholicism. On July 19, 1924, he wrote to Ezra Pound during the Fiesta of San Fermín in Pamplona, Spain. He told Pound, "I prayed to St. Fermin for you. Not that you needed it but I found myself in Mass with nothing to do and so prayed for my kid, for Hadley, for myself and your concert."[8]

Then on January 2, 1926, Ernest wrote to Ernest Walsh, saying, "If I am anything I am a Catholic. Had extreme unction administered to me as such in July, 1918 and recovered. So guess I am a super-catholic. . . . Am not what is called a 'good' catholic. . . . But cannot imagine taking any other religion seriously."[9] Though it's impossible to know exactly what occurred in Italy between Ernest and the priest, the results of the April 25, 1927, canonical inquest into Ernest's standing in the Catholic Church by the Archdiocese of Paris prior to his marriage to Pauline reported that he was "certified a Catholic in good standing."[10]

Despite the blessing of the Church and his apparent attraction to Pauline, however, Ernest was not without remorse for leaving Hadley. Later in life he would say, "I wish I had died before I ever loved anyone but her."[11] Similarly, the fourteen short stories collected in *Men without Women*, published in October 1927, four months after he married Pauline, reveal his preoccupation with failed relationships and marriages or, as literary critic Edmund Wilson would say, "a world where much is suffered."[12]

The people, places, and experiences Ernest encountered in Italy and France had worked to develop his worldview and style of writing. In Europe he found his voice by using people and places he had experienced to develop plots that focused on life in a post–World War I world and created a code for living in a godless world with grace under pressure. His Paris mentors helped him to write lean prose and dialogue that was described by the reviewers of *The Sun Also Rises* as "brilliant."[13]

Now with the success of *The Sun Also Rises* and his marriage to Pauline, he began to think he was finished with Europe. Once again, he wanted to leave home, but this time to go to America to write a book about what happened there. Though his "Oak Park novel" was never completed, the move to America was and conveniently coincided with Pauline's pregnancy and her desire to have her baby in the States. In March 1928, Ernest and Pauline sailed on the *Orita* from La Rochelle, France, to Havana, Cuba, and from there took a ferry to Key West, Florida.

Ernest's Key West attraction was fueled by John Dos Passos's stories of hitchhiking through the tropical island that stretched into the Caribbean from the Florida peninsula. The six weeks Ernest and Pauline intended to spend in Key West turned into twelve years. Still handsome, but now successful and even more confident, Ernest made friends easily. They were not the literary influences that nurtured his talent in Paris, but rather colorful characters he met on the docks and in the bars. Bahamian-born Bra Saunders taught Ernest deep-sea fishing; Joe Russell, owner of Sloppy Joe's bar and a Prohibition rum smuggler, became a loyal fishing companion; while Charles Thompson, whose wealth was derived from marine hardware and a fleet of fishing vessels, eventually became his African safari companion. Very quickly, Ernest fell into a routine. There was intense work during the early morning hours, life on the water in the afternoons, and, at sundown, talking with sailors, fishermen, and Cuban millionaires at the long front-to-rear bar at Sloppy Joe's. The handsome writer with the engaging smile and growing fame quickly made Key West his new home.

Calling Key West "the best place I've ever been any time anywhere,"[14] Ernest encouraged his closest friends to join him on the exotic, tropical island he found so conducive to work and play. Gerald and Sara Murphy, Archibald and Ada MacLeish, John and Katy Dos Passos, and Max Perkins were some of the early visitors. When French-speaking Bumby arrived from Paris, the poet Evan Shipman, Ernest's friend from the Closerie des Lilas, joined the household as Bumby's tutor.

Perhaps more surprising was a visit from Clarence and Grace Hemingway, who also were in Florida to check on their real estate investments. Ernest met his parents at the Key West dock and then introduced them to Pauline. Though Clarence was in poor health and worried about his real estate investments, the visit went well. Given Pauline's pregnancy, there were discussions and later an exchange of letters regarding where the new baby should be delivered. Ernest wrote to his father about the prospects of the baby being born in Michigan. Clarence advised against it, but offered "his services" to attend Pauline at Oak Park Hospital.[15] In the end, Patrick Hemingway was delivered by Cesarean section in Kansas City on June 28, 1928.

Ernest and Pauline had a healthy nine-pound son, but Ernest wrote to Max Perkins that Pauline had "a very bad time"[16] and later told Guy Hickok that "they finally had to open Pauline up like a picador's horse to lift out Patrick."[17] Both before and after Patrick's birth, Ernest was feverishly working on A Farewell to Arms. Given Ernest's habit of writing about what he knew, Patrick's birth no doubt influenced the graphic description of Catherine's Cesarean section at the end of the novel.

Though Ernest tried to maintain his work ethic and rituals of writing, there were many distractions—a new baby, a hunting trip to Wyoming with wartime friend Bill Horne, a visit by Bumby, and then on December 6, 1928, the suicide of his father. Worried about family finances due to the Florida real estate investments as well as his deteriorating health due to diabetes, Clarence shot himself in the head in the master bedroom of the home on Kenilworth Avenue with his father's, Anson's, Smith and Wesson revolver.

Upon receiving the news of his father's death, Ernest immediately went to Oak Park. His actions at this time of this crisis reveal his values and his often debated feelings toward his family. He began by indoctrinating his little brother, Leicester, in the rules of the Code and behaving with "grace under pressure." He told Leicester, "At the funeral, I want no crying. You understand, kid? There will be some others who will weep, and let them. But not in our family."[18]

Ernest's letters reveal his affection toward both of his parents as well as his sense of responsibility as the new man of the family. After the funeral he wrote to F. Scott Fitzgerald to thank him for loaning him money to get to Oak Park, saying, "My Father shot himself as I suppose you may have read in the papers. . . . I was fond as hell of my father and feel too punk—also sick etc.—to write a letter but wanted to thank you."[19] Then in a letter to Max Perkins, he expressed his sense of responsibility toward his mother as well as his work ethic: "My father shot himself—I was very fond of him and feel like hell about it. Got to Oak Park in plenty of time to handle things. . . . Realize of course that thing for me to do is not worry but get to work—finish my book properly so I can help them out with the proceeds."[20] The proceeds Ernest references were to provide his mother with a secure future. In another letter, he tells her, "Never worry because I will always fix things up—can always borrow money—if I haven't it. So don't ever worry, but go ahead with good confidence and get things going. . . . Remember you are on your own, but have a powerful backer—To whit me."[21]

The arrangements in anticipation of the Kenilworth Avenue house being sold also reveal Ernest's lifelong fascination with war. The correspondence between Ernest and his mother indicates that he wanted his grandfather Anson's .32-caliber Smith and Wesson "Long John" Civil War revolver—the suicide gun—and that she sent it to him. He also requested his mother to put "my [war] trophies . . . in a trunk or box and store them if you sell the house as I value them very much for Bumby."[22]

Finally, after the ordeal of Patrick's birth and his father's death, he just wanted to retreat to nature in the comfort of male companions. Since his boyhood days in Michigan, Ernest always assembled a loyal group of male companions for activity and adventure. The pattern began with fishing in Michigan and was transferred to bull-fights in Spain, deep-sea fishing in the Gulf Stream, and later hunting in Wyoming and Idaho. Now he begged Max Perkins to come to Key West, saying, "The Gulf Stream is alive with fish—really,"[23] and told John Dos Passos, "For God's sake come down. . . . Tarpon are in and have caught two."[24]

While Ernest enjoyed visits from valued friends, great fishing, and regular summer excursions to the Big Horn Mountains of Wyoming, Pauline, who was pregnant again, was learning to endure life in a subtropical "paradise." Key West was hot, humid, and filled with its share of small, run-down houses and salty, if not unsavory, sailors and fishermen. After living in a series of rented apartments, Pauline found a house that could be renovated as a peaceful, sophisticated home for her family. Thanks to Uncle Gus, Ernest, Pauline, Patrick, and newborn Gregory moved to 907 Whitehead Street in December 1931.

Built in 1851, the house needed repair but had the potential of being a charming home for the growing Hemingway family. Typical of Spanish Colonial–style, the house had wrought-iron railings encircling both the first and second floors, high ceilings, and shuttered windows. Almost every room looked out on the lush garden filled with fig, banyan, and lime trees. Built long before the days of air conditioning, the high ceilings and vertically aligned windows helped to keep the house cool. Because Key West did not have access to fresh water until 1941, the metal roof enabled the collection of rainwater, which was stored in a cistern. The ground floor contained a spacious living room, dining room, and kitchen. Upstairs there were bedrooms. Of great interest too was the carriage house that would be transformed into a secluded library and study for Ernest.

After Uncle Gus purchased the house for $8,000, Pauline oversaw extensive restorations. She added crystal chandeliers to the living room, dining room, and master bedroom; enhanced the walkways with decorative tiles; and then had her furniture shipped from Paris.

While Pauline restored and decorated the main house, Ernest transformed the carriage house into a setting that would become characteristic of his favorite places to work. It was a quiet retreat,

The 907 Whitehead Street House in Key West, Florida. *Hemingway Collection, John F. Kennedy Presidential Library and Museum*

away from the activity of the main house and accessed by a catwalk. The walls of the study were lined with bookshelves, and the room contained a round table, a leather-covered cigar factory stick chair, a typewriter, and eventually his hunting trophies. There Ernest would begin writing as early in the morning as possible, continue for six hours, and then, after the noon meal, join friends for life on the water and the excitement, challenges, and physical endurance that came from deep-sea fishing.

The years in Key West were fertile ones. Here he wrote *A Farewell to Arms* (1929), *Death in the Afternoon* (1932), *Green Hills of Africa* (1935), and *To Have and Have Not* (1937) and began *For Whom the Bell Tolls*. In Paris Ernest had found his voice by learning to write about his experiences. In Key West he tried to master it.

The success of *A Farewell to Arms* placed Ernest among the American literary masters. *Scribner's Magazine* serialized the work. Then the initial printing of more than thirty-one thousand copies of

Ernest Hemingway's study above the carriage house in Key West, Florida. *N. Sindelar Collection*

the book sold immediately, and Paramount bought the movie rights. Though the book was banned in Boston, critics praised the work worldwide. The *New York Times Book Review* called it "a moving and beautiful book," and the *New York Sun* called the retreat from Caporetto "unforgettable." Most of all, Ernest received the praise he had longed for when his mother wrote, "It is the best you have done yet—and deserves the high praise it is receiving."[25]

Following the publication of *A Farewell to Arms* and the death of his father, Ernest, accompanied by Pauline, decided to travel back to Spain to study the bullfights. Ernest had seen violence and death in his own life and now wanted to explore the experience of his father's suicide as well as his studies of the bullring to examine the feelings and attitudes associated with facing death. *Death in the Afternoon* would be a nonfiction work that detailed a matador's skill in playing with death. It would reflect Ernest's belief that bullfighting was not just a sport, but rather a drama that combined athleticism with artistry.

In the book, Ernest explains that this dangerous art form known as a bullfight is created by the matador's ability to dare a bull to come closer and closer in the course of the fight. The emotion is given by the closeness with which the matador brings the bull past his body, and it is prolonged by the slowness with which he can execute the pass. As the drama unfolds, "He [the matador] gives the feeling of his immortality, and, as you watch it, it becomes yours."[26]

After Ernest completed the research and initial drafts of the book, Ernest and Pauline returned to America on the *Ile de France* in September 1931. Ernest planned to finish his book in Key West, and Pauline planned to prepare for the birth of their second child. Both of them accomplished their goals. Pauline gave birth to Gregory Hancock Hemingway by Cesarean section after a twelve-hour labor on November 12, 1931, and *Death in the Afternoon* was published on September 23, 1932. The baby was a healthy nine-pound boy with big feet. The book received mixed reviews. While *Death in the Afternoon* was, and still remains, a scholarly treatise on the art of bullfighting and is filled with the vivid descriptions characteristic of Ernest's writing, the book's focus was a blood sport many readers found disgusting or of little interest.

Ernest and Pauline Hemingway at a bullfight in Spain, circa 1931. *Hemingway Collection, John F. Kennedy Presidential Library and Museum*

Feeling restless and disappointed with the reviews of *Death in the Afternoon*, Ernest began spending more and more time on the water. Ernest already was attracted to Cuba. It was only ninety miles from Key West, surrounded by waters abundant with fish and populated by people and a culture that were warm and nurturing. Having met Grant and Jane Mason, who lived near Havana, on board the *Ile de France*, he began spending time with Jane Mason. . She was strawberry blonde and twenty-two and enjoyed deep-sea fishing, pigeon shooting, and big game hunting.

Room 511 in the Ambos Mundos Hotel in Havana became yet another home for Ernest. While Jane occasionally visited Ernest and Pauline in Key West, bringing live flamingos and other exotic house gifts, Ernest began to spend months at a time in Cuba. Though Pauline would visit for two- or three-week periods, mostly she was at home with Patrick, now three, and the new baby. While Pauline experimented with new hair colors and attempted to make herself more attractive, it was about this time that Ernest began to refer to Pauline as POM, Poor Old Mama.

Jane Mason with Carlos Gutierrez aboard Sloppy Joe Russell's *Anita*. *Heming-way Collection, John F. Kennedy Presidential Library and Museum*

The Ambos Mundos Hotel, Havana, Cuba. *N. Sindelar Collection*

For a long time, Ernest had talked of a safari in Africa, and for a variety of reasons, Pauline fully supported the trip. As Pauline suspected, and probably hoped, Ernest's characteristic energy and work ethic would be diverted away from Jane Mason and Cuba and toward the execution of a new adventure. Her instincts were right. His safari planning included purchasing a high-powered, custom-made Springfield rifle with a telescope; watching a rehearsal of lion tamer Clyde Beatty to study the crouching and springing action of lions; and engaging Philip Percival, who had hunted with Winston Churchill and Teddy Roosevelt, as a guide.

On August 7, 1933, Ernest, Pauline, and Charles Thompson left for East Africa with Uncle Gus underwriting the $25,000 adventure for Ernest and Pauline. Traveling across the Serengeti Plain under the snowcapped Mt. Kilimanjaro, Ernest shot four lions, two

Ernest Hemingway with a rhinoceros on his 1933–1934 African safari. *Hemingway Collection, John F. Kennedy Presidential Library and Museum*

Ernest Hemingway with antelope and gazelle trophies on his 1933–1934 African safari. *Hemingway Collection, John F. Kennedy Presidential Library and Museum*

leopards, and thirty-five hyenas, as well as a number of cheetahs, a roan antelope, and numerous gazelles. The planning paid off as the prizes of the trip included not only the hunting trophies, but also a set of impressions and experiences (including amebic dysentery) that were recorded in articles sent back to *Esquire* and in the pages of "The Snows of Kilimanjaro," "The Short Happy Life of Francis Macomber," and *Green Hills of Africa*.

As usual, Ernest wrote from experience. The *Esquire* articles promoted Hemingway the legendary sportsman, who chronicled the quality and quantity of the African game and recorded for his American readers the herds of animals migrating across the Serengeti Plain along with the companion populations of hyenas and vultures.

However, the short stories, "The Short Happy Life of Francis Macomber" and "The Snows of Kilimanjaro," though set in Africa, were more of a reflection of the author's experiences with the pitfalls of married life. Francis Macomber, an accomplished hunter, holds a number of fishing records, but he does not have the respect of his wife. She views him as a coward when he runs from a lion and feeds on his weaknesses. Ernest portrays their marriage as one of demeaning convenience. The husband passively accepts his wife's wealth as well as her infidelities, while the wife accepts the fact that she no longer is attractive enough to better her position in life with a different partner.

Similarly, "The Snows of Kilimanjaro" also is set in Africa and focuses on two people trapped in an unhappy marriage. Harry is a writer, dying of gangrene, and his wealthy and once beautiful and sexually attractive wife becomes the victim of his caustic comments fueled by a lifetime of regrets. Unlike Ernest's Code Heroes, Harry faces death but does not exhibit "grace under pressure." He's un-heroic because he has sold out to a "rich bitch,"[27] telling her, "Your damned money was my armor."[28] Both short stories reveal the nega-tive aspects of marriage to a rich wife and contemplate the process of a graceless death.

The book, Green Hills of Africa, also focuses on the experiences of the trip and describes the beauty of the African landscape and the quality of the game. The careful, accurate descriptions that appear in Green Hills of Africa not only reflect the influence on economy of style nurtured by Ernest's Paris mentors, but also the earlier influ-ences of his paternal grandmother and his father. Adelaide Heming-way was an avid, degreed botanist who taught her grandchildren to see the details in nature. Marcelline once explained that pointing to a flower, Adeaide would say, "But do you really see it?"[29] Then, pointing out the specific details of the stamen and pistil, she created a totally different, more specific image for her grandchildren.

Dr. Hemingway also trained his children to see the details of nature. He regularly took his children on nature walks in the woods near the Oak Park houses and practiced the exacting art of taxidermy on his hunting trophies. As a result, grandparents, parents, Paris mentors (including the French Impressionist painters), and an exhil-arating trip to Africa all contributed to the descriptions of animals as well as the experiences of an avid hunter searching for and meeting the challenges of big game hunting in Green Hills of Africa.

The success of the The Sun Also Rises and A Farewell to Arms increased Ernest's confidence as a writer. He knew the value of writing from personal experience, the impact of describing the "vulgar" and "sordid" people he had encountered, and the power of using dialogue to advance a plot. However, this self-confidence led him to make tangential literary pronouncements that obscured his descriptions and annoyed the critics. Laced throughout *Green Hills of Africa* are sidebar comments about writers.

> Emerson, Hawthorne, Whittier and Company . . . were gentlemen or wished to be. They were all very respectable. They did not use the words that people always have used in speech, the words that survive in language. Nor would you gather they had bodies. They had minds, yes. Nice, dry, clean minds.[30]

As a result, the *New York Times* summarized the book as "pretty evenly divided between big game lore and salon controversy."[31]

If Ernest's growing self-confidence as a literary authority was marked by his editorial comments in *Green Hills of Africa*, his growing self-confidence as an international figure also was apparent given the ease with which he now was entering the world of the rich and famous. During his childhood, Ernest had been a frequent passenger aboard the SS *Manitou*, which took Ernest and his family from Chicago to Harbor Springs, Michigan. The 274-foot vessel was known for her speed and luxury, and the voyages of his childhood gave Ernest an early introduction to the routines and proprieties of traveling by ship.

Traveling back to the States aboard the *Ile de France* in 1934, he met Marlene Dietrich. She had entered the ship's dining room, but resisted being seated because she did not want to be the thirteenth person at the table. Ernest reacted quickly by offering to be the fourteenth man at the table and began a long friendship with the star. He affectionately called her "The Kraut." Later she documented her own feelings in a *New York Herald Tribune* article, calling Ernest "the most fascinating man I know."[32]

Characteristic of many of his friendships, Ernest played the role of Marlene's teacher or mentor. She saw him as a "huge rock" and believed "if more people had friends like Ernest there would be fewer analysts."[33] Once torn with indecision about a lucrative job offer, he counseled her not to do what she sincerely didn't want to do, saying, "Never confuse movement with action."[34] Those five words provided the actress with a philosophy of life, just as the words and actions of the Code Heroes in Ernest's novels and short stories provided his readers with a set of rules for living in the post–World War I world.

Though Ernest was the teacher, Marlene was a keen student. She understood his rules for living, appreciated the various ways in which he put them into action, and understood that he "found time to do the things most men only dream about."[35] Talking about the most fascinating man she knew, she said he was "the most positive life force I have ever encountered."[36] Their friendship survived twenty-seven years—from the time they met until Ernest's death. It was nourished by long-distance phone calls, letters, transatlantic crossings aboard the same ships, dinners at 21 Club in New York, and meetings at the Ritz Hotel in Paris.

But the Kraut was only the beginning. There would be friendships with Ava Gardner, Rita Hayworth, Ingrid Berman, Gary Cooper, and others. The boy from Oak Park was quickly becoming a citizen of the world. Before he was forty, he had called Italy, France, Switzerland, Spain, Canada, and Key West home. He had friends around the world, many of whom considered him "most fascinating."

Once back in Key West, Ernest continued to seek adventure by expanding his ability to confront the challenges of deep-sea fishing by purchasing his own boat. Using the knowledge and experience gained fishing off of Joe Russell's *Anita*, he ordered a thirty-eight-foot cabin cruiser from the Wheeler Shipyard in Brooklyn. The $3,000 down payment for the $7,500 boat came from an advance from *Esquire* magazine for future articles.

Disappointed by the reviews of *Green Hills of Africa*, Ernest sought relief by directing his energy and work ethic toward the execution of details that would make a stock boat suitable for deep-sea fishing in the Gulf. He increased the size of the gas tank to seventy-five gallons and added two copper-lined fish boxes on the aft deck, a live fish well, and a second motor for trolling. He lowered the sheer by a foot and had the white paint burned off in order for the boat to be painted black. Three years later he would add a flying bridge over the cockpit.

Ernest named the boat *Pilar*, after the shrine of Our Lady of the Pillar (*Pilar* in Spanish) at Saragossa, Spain, where he had seen bullfights in 1926. It also was the name he used in cables to Pauline while still married to Hadley and the name he would have given to the daughter he never had. Writing to Mike Strater, he said,

> This boat is a marvel for fishing. Takes any sea comfortably and can turn on her tail to chase a fish. Can literally turn in her own

length. Comfortable to live on board, big galley, five big beds, damned roomy and a wonderful fishing machine.[37]

Ernest's enthusiasm for the boat was driven by the quality and quantity of fish he caught in the waters between Key West and Cuba. An avid letter writer, it follows he would keep a ship's log. Thus, true to his note-taking, letter-writing nature, the fishing logs record that during the month of May 1932, he landed nineteen marlin; that April to mid-July 1933, he brought in fifty-two marlin; and that he set a Cuban record by landing a 468-pound, thirteen-foot marlin.

However, Ernest's involvement with customizing the boat, his passion for deep-sea fishing, and his attraction to Jane Mason were temporary remedies to the growing depression of an author who had earned fame and success at an early age. The sales and reviews of *Death in the Afternoon* and *Green Hills of Africa* had been disappointing. He was writing articles for *Esquire* and political com-

Ernest Hemingway's thirty-eight-foot Wheeler powerboat, *Pilar*, circa 1934. During World War II, the boat patrolled the waters near Cuba for German submarines. *Hemingway Collection, John F. Kennedy Presidential Library and Museum*

Ernest Hemingway with a marlin, Havana Harbor, 1934. *Hemingway Collection, John F. Kennedy Presidential Library and Museum*

mentary for *New Masses* rather than feverishly working on the next novel. And he appears to have lost interest in his wife, who was told by her doctors not to have more babies but refused to practice birth control due to her strict Catholicism.

Harry in "The Snows of Kilimanjaro" was literally rotting away from gangrene, but Harry's condition and words of regret may have just reflected Ernest's midlife, midcareer fears. Was he truly afraid of nothing, or was he afraid that he too was rotting away under the protective shield of Pauline's wealth? Trips to Spain and safaris to Africa had been exciting diversions from the comfortable Key West life, but they had not produced the quality of thought and the preciseness of writing that were the result of the earlier relationships and experiences encountered in Italy, France, and Spain. Now he had a host of friends, wealthy, famous, and influential. They admired his daring adventures, his literary fame, and his good-natured storytelling. However, in a letter to Matthew Josephson, he admitted he had a nice boat and a beautiful house in Key West, but summarized his life by saying, "I could stay on here forever, but it's a soft life. Nothing's really happening to me here and I've got to get out."[38]

His escape route was charted by a young blonde writer named Martha Gellhorn. The destination was Spain.

Chapter Four

The Escape to War

You can't preserve your happiness by . . . putting it away in moth balls.

—Ernest Hemingway to the Pfeiffer family, 1937[1]

Ernest Hemingway as a war correspondent for NANA during the Spanish Civil War, circa 1936. *Hemingway Collection, John F. Kennedy Presidential Library and Museum*

ERNEST'S FASCINATION WITH BULLFIGHTING and his many trips to Spain made him sensitive to Spain's political environment. As he had predicted, a civil war broke out there in 1936. When that happened, he felt the same call to action he experienced when he was eighteen and wanted to leave Kansas City and go to Italy. Only now he wanted to go to Spain; he needed to be part of the action. To his delight, and Pauline's dismay, he accepted an offer from the North American Newspaper Alliance (NANA) to cover the war in Spain.

Leaving Key West was a remedy for the routine he could not tolerate. He recognized that both his life and writing needed action. Family life had become too comfortable, and he knew the adventures of big game hunting and deep-sea fishing were somewhat calculated diversions. The world was in a depression. Yet life in Key West allowed his disengagement from this economic and social crisis as well as the time and money to pursue bullfighting, big game hunting, and deep-sea fishing. While he was pursuing his personal adventures or telling stories at the bar at Sloppy Joe's, his literary contemporaries were writing about political and social causes.

The hurricane that hit the Upper and Lower Matecumbe Keys in September 1935 was particularly disillusioning to him and was perhaps a call to action. Hundreds of out-of-work veterans who were building a highway that would connect the Florida Keys were killed. Ernest visited the area after the hurricane was over and blamed the Roosevelt administration for not getting the veterans off the islands in time. The images of the destruction brought back the indignity of death he had witnessed in World War I. He told Max Perkins, "Saw more dead than I'd seen in one place since the lower Piave in June of 1918."[2] The washed-away rail lines, the leveled buildings, and the human loss became fodder for a scathing article he wrote for the *New Masses*. "Who Murdered the Vets?" was quoted in *Time* and marked, for some, Ernest's indictment of the New Deal, which had sent hundreds of Civilian Conservation Corps workers into hot, humid conditions with poor food, flimsy houses, and inadequate medical care.

By the time he was thirty-six, life's experiences in Key West, as well as Oak Park and Paris, had shown Ernest the differences between the rich, the poor, and those in between. The Oak Park of his youth was filled with Republicans, and Grandfather Anson was proud to say that "he would never knowingly sit at a table with a Democrat."[3] Yet Ernest's family was more involved with service to God and their country than with partisan politics or social pretensions. Both grandfathers served in the Civil War, and Dr. Hemingway was devoted to his medical practice and the natural world of Walloon Lake. If any family member had social aspirations, it was Grace, who was proud of her English heritage and observed Boxing Day as a regular Christmas tradition. Yet she too was focused on raising well-educated children and enabled their love of the outdoors by endorsing the regular summer vacations to Walloon Lake.

Throughout his early life, Ernest's personal adventures and writing reflected his family's love of the outdoors and their belief in a strong work ethic. His early experiences with Indians in Michigan helped him to embrace a sense of self-reliance and admire the simple beauty of the natural world. His boyhood experiences gave him the skills as well as the tenacity to explore life in the mountains above Lake Geneva (Lac Leman), pursue deep-sea fishing in the Gulf Stream, and survive in a tent while pursuing big game in Africa. His belief in the value of hard work contributed to his early success as a writer. Combined with his self-confidence, he didn't give up but rather adhered to a strict work schedule and what would become a lifelong ritual for the process of writing. Living frugally, he used the Paris years to cull content from his personal experiences and hone his craft as a writer.

Then he was seduced by money. After the success of *The Sun Also Rises* and *A Farewell to Arms*, Ernest increasingly associated with celebrities and people of wealth. In Paris, Ernest met F. Scott Fitzgerald, who thought "the very rich are different from you and me"; traveled with Gerald and Sara Murphy; and fell in love with Pauline.

In Key West he accepted the soft life provided by Pauline and her household staff; the house, car, and African safari provided by Uncle Gus; and the freedom to write without really having to worry about providing for his wife and children. His early interests in hunting and fishing evolved into adventures that required money and leisure time, and he began to spend more and more time in the company of the rich. Though he believed that wealth often corrupted writers and often spoke badly of the rich, he still enjoyed their company and their pastimes.

However, treatment of veterans working in the Upper and Lower Matecumbe Keys and the poverty brought on by the Depression penetrated the bubble of comfortable isolation Ernest was enjoying in Key West. Once a quiet fishing village, Key West now was populated by federal bureaucrats who were using Federal Emergency Relief Act (FERA) funds to promote tourism.

Ernest's growing awareness of financial and social strata is reflected in *To Have and Have Not*. The characters are based on people he met in Key West—the working class he encountered on the docks and at Sloppy Joe's, the rich who moored their boats in Key West harbor, and the illegal Chinese immigrants who were being smuggled from Cuba to Key West to promote tourism in newly formed Chinatowns. The working men, such as the main character Harry Morgan, are decent people who care about their families and are willing to work to support them, but are driven to desperate, violent, and sometimes criminal actions because of the Depression. When a wealthy customer does not pay Harry's charter boat fee, Harry is forced to take Chinese immigrants from Cuba to Florida. The illegal action is justified because "I've got family"[4] and "I'm broke."[5]

While the "have nots" are presented with sympathy and understanding, the "haves" are portrayed as insensitive opportunists. Some have made their fortunes in businesses similar to Uncle Gus's Sloan's Liniment enterprise, "selling something everybody used by the millions of bottles, which cost three cents a quart to make."[6] Others, such as Harry Carpenter, live on trust funds and will survive even if they are "dropped from 5500 feet without a parachute" because they will "land safely with [their] knees under some rich man's table."[7]

In *To Have and Have Not*, Ernest's disgust with FERA and the Roosevelt administration propels him into social commentary. Depression-era Key West is no longer a quiet fishing village, but rather a land of inequality and corruption, where the pleasure-seeking "haves" take advantage of the "have nots." Mrs. Laughton looks longingly at Harry Morgan and tells her husband to "buy me that." Similarly, "the yellow rat-eating aliens" are smuggled into the States to populate Chinatowns to promote the tourism of wealthy thrill-seekers curious about Orientalism.

As with other novels, Ernest used his personal experiences and friendships to develop content for *To Have and Have Not*. His marriage to Pauline and his travels with the Fitzgeralds and Murphys gave him new insights into the thoughts and habits of the rich. The emotional and financial support provided by Uncle Gus gave him an understanding of the protection and security that accompanies life with a trust fund. Though he shares his thoughts about the distribution of wealth, *To Have and Have Not* offers no solutions. The plot of the novel seems to argue for social and political changes to help the working man, but the New Deal remedies were not a solution for Ernest. He believed the New Deal reforms asked people to do hard work for insufficient pay while robbing them of their dignity. As a result, the fate of Harry Morgan, the novel's main character, outlines the limits of personal freedom and self-reliance and the absence of grace under pressure in Depression-era Key West. However, the closest Ernest comes to a solution is for Harry to say, "No matter how a man alone ain't got no f—— chance."[8]

The death and destruction of Lower Matecumbe Key after the 1935 hurricane. *Hemingway Collection, John F. Kennedy Presidential Library and Museum.*

Ernest Hemingway and others aboard Sloppy Joe Russell's *Anita*, 1932–1933.
Hemingway Collection, John F. Kennedy Presidential Library and Museum

Ernest's concern about the country's basic values and his personal conflict over money were real and troubling to him. His personal solution was to leave Key West, reemerge himself in a life of action, and return to war.

In December 1936, Martha Gellhorn entered Sloppy Joe's. At twenty-eight, the attractive blonde had already traveled extensively in Spain, France, and Germany and had written articles for the *New Republic*, the *St. Louis Post-Dispatch*, and the Paris edition of *Vogue*. She too was from St. Louis, where her father had been an obstetrician. Yet, despite the obvious similarities of being the child of an obstetrician as was Ernest, being from St. Louis and having attended Bryn Mawr as did Hadley, and having spent time in Paris working for *Vogue* as did Pauline, the real attraction was Ernest and Martha's mutual interest in the political climate of Spain.

When they met, Madrid was under siege and atrocities were being committed by both the Loyalists and the Nationalists. Ernest's eagerness to get back into the action and Martha's desire to report on the action firsthand created a bond between them. They talked all afternoon at Sloppy Joe's while Pauline awaited Ernest's arrival for a dinner with guests. Eventually, Pauline sent Charles Thompson to fetch Ernest, but Thompson returned, saying that Ernest had been delayed by "a beautiful blonde in a black dress."[9]

During the spring and fall of 1937, Ernest made four trips to Spain as a war correspondent for NANA and engaged in a life of risk with Martha. The Spanish Civil War pitted the Loyalists, who were supported by the Russians, against Franco's Nationalists, who were supported by Hitler and Mussolini. Ernest supported the Loyalist cause because he believed it would bring a better life to the ordinary people of Spain and because the Nationalists were supported by the Fascists. His dislike of Fascism went back to 1922 when he first reported on Mussolini's rise to power and called him "the biggest bluff in Europe."[10] Martha too supported the Loyalist cause and participated in Ernest's most dangerous assignments. They were living in Madrid, a city under assault, and each day was filled with danger and death in the streets. Writers and journalists from around the world converged on the scene. Andre Malraux, W. H. Auden, and Stephen Spender were there to support the cause as was James Lardner, the son of Ring Lardner, whom Ernest had admired and imitated during his days as a student in Oak Park.

The energy and excitement of the war, his interest in Martha, and the companionship and stimulation from fellow writers mirrored the productive times Ernest spent in Europe fifteen years earlier. But now Ernest was a writer with an extraordinary reputation and a visible, meaningful spokesman for the Loyalist cause. *Newsweek* published a story stating that his fee of one dollar per word was the highest ever paid a war correspondent, and his affiliation with NANA meant that his articles would circulate in some sixty newspapers, among them the *New York Times*, the *San Francisco Chronicle*, and the *Kansas City Star*. Herbert Matthews, a seasoned *New York Times* correspondent, praised Ernest's articles, saying that he represented "much that is brave and good and fine in a somewhat murky world."[11]

While Ernest craved the excitement and danger of the war, his decision to go to Spain reaffirmed some of his most basic values.

Central to his love for Spain was his love of the bullfight, which he first discovered with Robert McAlmon in 1923. For Ernest, a skilled matador possessed the values of manhood, honor, and self-reliance that had been embraced by Ernest's father and grandfathers, but discredited by World War I and, more recently, by the Depression. It was the courage, honor, and stoic acceptance of death that made matadors heroes in *The Sun Also Rises*, in contrast to the dissipated characters of the lost generation. Good matadors displayed grace under pressure and dignity in their acceptance of death and embraced the Spanish commonsense view of death as something neither fearful nor mystical.

Ernest had told Stephen Spender his principal reason for coming to Spain was to discover "whether he had lost his nerve under the conditions of warfare."[12] During the Spanish Civil War, Ernest proved to himself and others that he had not lost his nerve. What he wrote and what he did showed that he still was studying grace under pressure—in himself as well as others. He relished the role of the old war veteran and sought situations to test his courage. He repeatedly exposed himself to enemy fire and often called attention to the risks he was taking to get his stories, saying, "This correspondent has been doing the most dangerous thing you can do in this war. That is, keep close behind an unstabilized line where the enemy is attacking with mechanized forces."[13]

His assignments as a war correspondent were similar to the ones he did for the *Toronto Star* in the early 1920s. NANA gave him a great deal of freedom to focus on feature and background stories rather than being responsible for hard news. He was genuinely outraged by the Fascist disregard for civilian lives and wrote vivid descriptions of the suffering of innocent bystanders to stimulate similar outrage in his readers. His articles detailed his disgust with the Fascists for preying on innocent victims, and one article spoke of the scattered bodies of women who had been waiting in line for soap and a streetcar filled with workers that had been struck by a nine-inch shell.

In his April 11, 1937, NANA dispatch, he wrote about the shelling of Madrid and detailed not only the "legitimate" shelling of military targets, but also the shelling of innocent Sunday promenaders: "They killed an old woman returning from market dropping her in a huddled black heap of clothing, with one leg, suddenly detached, whirling against the wall of an adjoining house."[14] In the same article he describes a car being hit, and "the driver lurch[ing] out, his scalp hanging down over his eyes, to sit down on the side with his hand against his face, the blood making a smooth sheen down over his chin."[15]

Reminiscent of the articles he wrote for the *Toronto Star* during the Greco-Turkish War in 1922, he also showed great sympathy for the refugees who were driven from their homes by the war. In "The Flight of the Refugees," he tells of a woman riding a mule

> holding a still freshly red-faced baby that could not have been two days old. The mother's head swung steadily up and down with the motion of the beast she rode, and the baby's jet-black hair was drifted gray with the dust. A man led the mule forward. . . . "When was the baby born?" I asked him as our car swung alongside. "Yesterday," he said proudly.[16]

Coached by his grandfathers, he believed the strain and horror of battle tested the individual and brought out the best and worst in men. Men in the midst of battle became the characters for some of his greatest fiction because in war men could demonstrate honor, courage, and grace under pressure. His experiences in World War I were the basis for *A Farewell to Arms*. Though Frederic Henry is blown up while eating cheese, the reader learns from Frederic's actions and code of behavior. He carries out his orders, fulfills his duties, and believes the Italians should keep fighting because "defeat is worse."[17] When Frederic makes his separate peace and jumps into the river to escape the senseless actions of the carabinieri, it's more an act of common sense than one of desertion.

Similarly, Ernest's friendships and personal experiences in the Spanish Civil War served to create memorable characters in *For Whom the Bell Tolls*. Robert Jordan is modeled after Robert Merriman, an American professor who left his research on collective farming in Russia to become a commander in the Abraham Lincoln Brigade and was killed during the final assault on Belchite. Maria is based on a young nurse of the same name who was gang-raped by Nationalist soldiers early in the war. The novel's three days of conflict takes place near the El Tajo gorge that cuts through the Andalusian town of Ronda, where a political massacre like the one led by Pablo occurred early in the Spanish Civil War.

In the novel, as in the war, the Fascists prevail. At the climax of the novel, Robert Jordan prepares for his own death as the Fascist cavalrymen approach. He is injured but has a submachine gun and waits to engage the enemy so that they have no choice but to shoot him. Given the choice between death or capture and torture, Jordan is a model of grace under pressure. He knows, "I have fought for what I believed in for a year now. If we win here we will win everywhere. The world is a fine place and worth the fighting for and I hate very much to leave it."[18]

When it became apparent that the Fascists would win in Spain, NANA released Ernest from his assignment. He returned to Havana in 1939 convinced the Spanish Civil War was merely a prelude to a larger global conflict. His instincts were correct. He began writing *For Whom the Bell Tolls* in March 1939, and six months later Nazi Germany invaded Poland, initiating the beginning of World War II. *For Whom the Bell Tolls* was published in October 1940. By April 1941, almost five hundred thousand copies had been sold, and in January 1942, the movie rights were purchased by Paramount for $100,000.

Ernest returned to Havana when he left Spain. Though still married to Pauline, whose Catholicism delayed their divorce, he lived with Martha at the Hotel Biltmore Sevilla in Havana. From there he commuted to Key West until November 1940, when Pauline finally divorced him on grounds of desertion. Ernest had been happy living at the Hotel Florida in Madrid, and before the divorce was comfortable at the Biltmore Sevilla while maintaining a façade of separation from Martha by posting and receiving mail at the Ambos Mundos. He enjoyed the atmosphere of Old Havana and the camaraderie he found at the bars of the Floridita and the Bogedita del Medio. His routine was intact. He'd write in the peace of his room in the morning and retreat to the bars or his boat in the afternoon.

Martha, however, found the hotel quarters cramped and decided to pursue a means to keep Ernest out of the local bars. Finca Vigia, Look-out Farm, met both of her objectives. The house needed work, but it had a swimming pool and a tennis court and was located a reasonable distance from Havana on fifteen acres of land. Though Ernest thought the rent of $100 a month was too much, they moved in and Martha began the renovation of the house. Two weeks after his divorce from Pauline, he and Martha were married in Cheyenne, Wyoming. When they returned to Havana, Ernest bought the Finca for $18,500.

Though Ernest openly stated, "What I wanted was a wife in bed at night not somewhere having even higher adventures at so many thousand bucks the adventure,"[19] Martha's focus was on her career as a journalist. After they were married, Ernest joined her on her trip to China to cover the Sino-Japanese War and what she called a "working honeymoon." While she was being sent to cover the Sino-Japanese War for *Collier's*, Ernest arranged to write some articles for *PM*. However, they not only covered the Sino-Japanese War, but also collected intelligence for the U.S. government. They were asked to observe whether Chiang Kai-shek was using U.S. military aid to suppress Communism or for fighting the Japanese.

Ernest was able to meet with both Generalissimo Chiang Kai-shek and Communist leader Chou En-lai, though obviously not at the same time. Ernest's reports favored the anti-Communist Chiang, partly because Ernest respected him as a military leader who had put aside his war against the Communists in the interest of the bigger war against Japan.[20] When Ernest and Martha were debriefed at the Office of Naval Intelligence, Ernest emphasized the strategic importance of support to Chiang Kai-shek, believing that a long ground war in China would engage a majority of the Japanese army and delay their drive into Southeast Asia. He believed this strategy would give the United States time to build up a two-ocean navy that would be crucial to U.S. national defense.

Ernest's introductions to Chinese leaders and diplomats were facilitated by H. H. Kung, the finance minister of China. H. H. Kung was a friend of Ernest's uncle, Dr. Willoughby Hemingway, and married to Madame Chiang Kai-shek's sister. Uncle Willoughby had been a medical missionary in China and responsible for Kung attending Oberlin College. While in the States, both men had been guests at the Hemingway homes in Oak Park. Because of Kung's

Ernest and Martha Gellhorn Hemingway on their "working honeymoon" in China, 1941. *Hemingway Collection, John F. Kennedy Library*

Ernest and Martha Hemingway with Madame Chiang Kai-shek, Chung King, China, 1941. *Hemingway Collection, John F. Kennedy Presidential Library and Museum*

connections, Ernest was able to meet not only with Generalissimo Chiang Kai-shek, but also with Chou En-lai, the Communist leader who was living underground because he feared the Generalissimo.

The working honeymoon met Ernest's needs for sleuthing and intelligence gathering and Martha's need to see the Asia she only had read about. However, a major difference between the newly married couple surfaced during the trip. Ernest accepted the poverty and squalor of China; Martha was appalled by it. Trying to stay clean, Martha bathed and brushed her teeth in the local water. As a result, her hands became infected with "China rot," a highly contagious fungus. The incident initiated a pattern of Ernest's annoyance with Martha's habits of cleanliness. He responded to the situation by saying, "Honest to God Martha, You brought this on yourself. I told you not to wash."[21]

When they returned to Cuba, Martha flew to London to cover World War II for *Collier's* and began a series of events where much of their married life was spent apart. Though Martha started the restoration of Finca Vigia, was a good stepmother to Ernest's three sons, and played the role of Mrs. Hemingway while in Cuba, she also was an avid journalist and preferred life on the road. As World War II continued to escalate, Martha pursued assignments in Europe for *Collier's*. When she was unable to gain accreditation as a war correspondent in a military zone, she took a *Collier's* assignment to report on German naval activity in the Caribbean while Ernest was in Cuba pursuing counterintelligence activities and patrolling the local waters for German U-boats.

Ernest's newest series of adventures came about because the American ambassador to Cuba, Spruille Braden, had become concerned about the loyalties of the three hundred thousand Spaniards living in Cuba. If Franco's Spain joined the Axis powers, which side of the war would the Cuban Spaniards support? Given Cuba's proximity to the United States, and its history of revolution, Braden decided to recruit Ernest for counterintelligence activities. He asked him to report on the actions and any sabotage attempts of the pro-Nazi Falange, which was threatening to U.S. interests. Ernest eagerly accepted the assignment and recruited a bizarre group of "secret agents," and the "Crook Factory" was born.

Later when German submarines were discovered in the Gulf of Mexico, Ernest was granted permission to use the *Pilar* for coastal patrol and investigative work on the south coast of Cuba. He transformed the *Pilar* into a spy ship camouflaged as a marine research vessel. The *Pilar* carried bazookas, explosives, machine guns, and radio equipment. Ernest hoped the *Pilar* would be halted by a German sub so the *Pilar* crew could attack the German crew with machine-gun fire and destroy the sub with blasts from bazookas and by throwing hand grenades down the conning tower. Though Ernest never carried out the plan, and Martha saw it as a mere ploy to get more rationed gasoline for the boat, the *Pilar* did report useful information to the navy, which bombed and presumably sank several subs in the waters off Cuba.

Martha's letters to Ernest during this period reveal that she begged him to join her in Europe to share in the adventures of World War II. When he finally did go to London, *Collier's* made Ernest the leading correspondent in place of Martha. Ambitious and hardworking, Martha was furious, and the end of their marriage was in sight. Ironically, they had agreed on large political issues and taken life-threatening risks before they were married, but were too competitive to live together as a happily married couple. In addition to competing for the best stories, they bickered over little things. Ernest told his friend A. E. Hotchner that "she liked everything sanitary. Her father was a doctor so she made our house look as much like a hospital as possible. No animal heads no matter how beautiful, because they were unsanitary."[22]

Once Ernest was back in Europe, what had become predictable patterns in his life reemerged. He became involved in the war and was discovered by the woman who would become his fourth wife. The success of *For Whom the Bell Tolls* and the articles he had written for NANA during the Spanish Civil War gave him a voice of authority and leverage as a war correspondent. In a September 1935 article for *Esquire*, "Notes of the Next War: A Serious Topical Letter," he had predicted World War II, but argued that the United

States should not get involved. The article reflected his early values, nurtured by his grandfathers, saying, "In the old days it was sweet and fitting to die for one's country."[23] Then the lessons learned in World War I appear.

> But in modern war there is nothing sweet nor fitting in your dying. You will die like a dog for no good reason. . . . Before the war you always think that it's not you that dies. But you will die, brother, if you go to it long enough.[24]

His final advice to American readers was "We were fools to be sucked in once on a European war and we should never be sucked in again."[25]

Though his prediction about the coming war was correct and his advice valid, once back in Europe as a war correspondent, Ernest once again placed himself in dangerous situations to be part of the action and absorb the experiences needed for a good story. From the vantage point aboard a landing craft off the coast of Normandy, he witnessed the D-Day landing at Omaha Beach. In his "Voyage to Victory" article for the Collier's July 22, 1944, edition, he described for his readers the steep cliffs of Omaha Beach, the vantage points of the German machine guns along the lower ridges of the cliffs, and the drowning of hundreds of men as they tried to reach the shore under heavy machine-gun fire. He admitted that

> real war is never like paper war nor do accounts of it read much the way it looks. But if you want to know how it was in an LCV(P) on D-Day when we took Fox Green Beach and Easy Red beach on the sixth of June, 1944, then this is as near as I can come to it.[26]

After the D-Day invasion, Ernest set up headquarters at the Hotel du Grand Veneur in Rambouillet outside of Paris. War correspondents were not allowed to bear arms or participate in military action, but Ernest convinced Colonel David Bruce to give him authorization to participate in military intelligence activities. The Germans were approaching and the consensus was they would take the town of Rambouillet that night. Given his instinct for strategy and sleuthing, he took over intelligence operations regarding German activity on the road to Paris. Using English, French, and broken

German, he interrogated German deserters and prisoners as they were brought in and provided information to the U.S. military on roadblocks, radar installations, and anti-aircraft defenses between Rambouillet and Paris. Though his take-charge attitude and actions annoyed other war correspondents, Ernest later boasted that his operations were "straight out of Mosby," the celebrated guerrilla leader of the U.S. Civil War.[27] David Bruce, the OSS officer who authorized his position at Rambouillet, later said,

> I entertain a great admiration for [Ernest] not only as an artist and friend, but as a cool, resourceful, imaginative military tactician and strategist. He unites, from what I saw of him, that rare combination of advised recklessness and caution that knows how to properly seize upon a favorable opportunity which, once lost, is gone forever. He was a born leader of men, and in spite of his strong independence of character, impressed me as a highly disciplined individual.[28]

Ernest Hemingway in Rambouillet, France, during World War II. *Hemingway Collection, John F. Kennedy Presidential Library and Museum*

Ernest Hemingway during World War II. *Hemingway Collection, John F. Kennedy Presidential Library and Museum.*

Throughout his life Ernest loved the action and exhilaration that came from the involvement with war. As time progressed, however, he saw more clearly the horror of battle and wrote not only about how it brought out the best and worst in men, but also how both sides in a war bore guilt. He had come to believe that it was impossible for a country to wage modern warfare and emerge with its innocence intact. Though a strong supporter of the Loyalists in the Spanish Civil War, he wrote about the atrocities that took place on both sides in *For Whom the Bell Tolls.* As an American citizen he first advised that the United States stay out of the conflict in Europe. Then after the country's World War II involvement and victory, he said, "We have fought this war and won it. Now let us not be sanctimonious nor hypocritical, nor vengeful nor stupid."[29] After his experiences in World War II, he believed the leaders of Nazi Germany should be punished, but he also believed "a country that killed 60,000 civilians with one atomic bomb had no reason to feel smug."[30]

Chapter Five

───────○───────

Settling Down

Everything I have is here—my pictures, my books, my good work place and good memories.

—Ernest Hemingway to A. E. Hotchner,
Finca Vigia, 1960[1]

Ernest Hemingway at Finca Vigia, San Francisco de Paula, Cuba, circa 1940. *Hemingway Collection, John F. Kennedy Presidential Library and Museum*

WHEN THE FIGHTING SUBSIDED AND PARIS WAS LIBERATED, Ernest did not report on General Dietrich von Choltitz's surrender at Gare Montparnasse or join the victory parade down the Champs-Elysees. Rather, he took his Jeep straight to his favorite hotel, the Ritz, and ordered champagne for everyone in the bar. Being a part of the liberation of Paris meant a lot to him. Prior to entering the city he recalled having "a funny choke in [his] throat and . . . [having] to clean [his] glasses because there now, below [him], gray and always beautiful, was spread the city [he had] loved best in all the world."[2]

Feeling sentimental, he knew his early years in Paris had been important to his development as a person and as a writer. When he first arrived in Paris, he and Hadley had lived frugally on the Left Bank. Now he was an acclaimed author and celebrated at the Ritz, where the hotel's founder had defined luxury by building marble bathrooms with huge bathtubs, inventing the king-sized bed, and staffing the dining room with waiters in white tie. Ernest once wrote to his friend A. E. Hotchner, "When I dream of afterlife in heaven, the action always takes place in the Paris Ritz."[3]

Back in Paris Ernest renewed old friendships and made new friends quickly. Based on their mutual interest in hunting and fishing, he developed a friendship with the founder's son, Charles Ritz. However, his time in Paris also was spent reminiscing and reconnecting with others. In many ways his life had come full circle. He began in Paris as an unknown writer, living simply and learning from others. Now his acclaim was worldwide, he was living in luxury, and others looked to him for advice and inspiration. At a party in Sylvia Beach's apartment, both Jean-Paul Sartre and Simone de Beauvoir observed that "many of the rules [they] observed in [their] novels were inspired by Hemingway."[4] In a nostalgic letter to Mary Welsh, he said, "Have been to all the old places I ever lived in Paris and everything is fine. But it is all so improbable that you feel like you have died and it is all a dream."[5]

While he worked hard for his success, many of his Paris friends had struggled too, but had not reaped the same rewards. He had a joyous reunion with Sylvia Beach, who had survived the occupation of France, but had needed to hide her books for fear of confiscation by the Germans. Then he learned that Gertrude Stein had hidden from the Germans in unoccupied France, but had been forced to sell her *Portrait of Madame Cezanne* in order to survive.

Ezra Pound, who had been so influential in refining Ernest's prose, had been accused of treason and declared mentally unsound and was living out thirteen years of incarceration and treatment as a mental patient. Ernest was fully aware of the contributions all these people had made to his life and to his writing and was grateful. When Pound was released, Ernest sent him a check for $1,000 to help him return to Italy. However, Pound never cashed the check, preferring to frame it.

Though Ernest and Martha were still married and occasionally crossed paths as correspondents reporting on the same battle, their marriage was basically over. Ernest's new interest was Mary Welsh Monks, who was a feature writer for *Time* and married to an Australian journalist. They met in London prior to the D-Day invasion, and after Ernest's luncheon proposal of "I don't know you, Mary, but I want to marry you," exchanged numerous letters.[6] Mary arrived in Paris and checked into the Ritz the day after Ernest arrived. Ernest was in Room 31; Mary was in Room 86. As their relationship developed, Ernest used his experiences with his three previous marriages to filter and judge the essential criteria for what would be his fourth and hopefully his final marriage.

Ernest's actions and letters reveal the values he was seeking in a new marriage. He was a compulsive note taker and habitual letter writer. He had kept careful records of Hadley's menstrual cycles, hoping to avoid having more children. Then he kept ship's logs aboard the *Pilar*, noting the number, type, and weight of the fish he caught. Later in life, concerned about his health, he recorded his weight and blood pressure on the painted walls of his bathroom at Finca Vigia. Throughout his career as a writer, he also kept notebooks on experiences and images that would eventually appear in his novels and short stories. He saved the notebooks, and the collection ranges from simple student *cahiers* from France to journals covered in zebra skins from Africa.

His numerous letters to friends, family, and editors seemed to have provided a release from the concentration of his serious writing. They are filled with opinions, humor, and four-letter words and at times are very loving or romantic. Letters seemed to have balanced his needs for work and play, his needs for serious writing and his needs for friendship and reflection.

He wrote to "Dearest Hadley" throughout his lifetime. These letters focused on their mutual love, concern, and support of Bumby, but also were filled with affection for her. As time progressed, his appreciation of the love and emotional and financial support she provided during the six years they were married grew. She later married Paul Mower, but Ernest continued to end his letters with warm sentiments, saying, "Much love to you and all my best to Paul. I admire you both very much."[7]

Pauline provided opportunities that helped to promote Ernest as a writer and a legend. Their marriage gave him the financial freedom to focus on his writing and the means to explore deep-sea fishing aboard the *Pilar* and big game hunting in Africa. Uncle Gus doted on Pauline and respected Ernest as a writer. Ernest's portrait held a prominent place in Uncle Gus's New York apartment, and Uncle Gus's broad-based financial support was a reflection of the enjoyment he received from enabling Ernest to write and engage in exotic adventures.

Though Ernest eventually felt the need to free himself from the soft life of Key West, there's no doubt that he appreciated the generous financial support of Pauline's family. Numerous letters reveal his gratitude for Christmas presents that allowed him to purchase more sophisticated steering controls for the *Pilar*, as well as birthday checks and contributions of stock to his children's trust funds. He appreciated too Pauline's well-staffed and well-organized household, telling his in-laws, "This place really runs very smoothly and we eat very well and we would love to see you."[8]

Though Ernest told the Pfeiffer family that "for a long time me and my conscience both have known I had to go to Spain,"[9] Martha's youthful attractiveness and keen interest in Spain was an important factor in Ernest's leaving Key West and going to Spain. Yet once the Spanish Civil War was over, so was Ernest and Martha's relationship. When they moved into the Finca, they learned that he liked trophies of animal heads, but she didn't; that her friends were clean and well groomed and that he preferred the fishermen he met on the docks and didn't care if his pals jumped into the pool without first taking a shower. Later he told Mary Welsh, he had had his "ration of Bryn Mawr, Bergdorf Goodman and the Lancaster."[10] He wrote to Patrick that he was "going to get me somebody who wants to stick around with me and let me be the writer of the family."[11] He deduced from his marital experiences that he did not want a professional rival such as Martha, but the support and stability of someone like Hadley and the household skills of someone like Pauline. Mary's conclusion was that she would need to give up her career and accept the fact that Ernest wanted a "practical nurse" for himself and his children.[12]

After three marriages, success as a novelist and war correspondent, and a growing reputation as an international sportsman, what Ernest wanted most was to return to Cuba and create a balanced life. The balance between work and play would include time for writing as well as time for his boys, time for fishing, and time for friends. It appeared that he was ready to settle down with Mary. While reporting on the bloody battle for the Hurtgen Forest as a war correspondent, he wrote to Mary and asked her to "think about the boat and the dark blue, almost purple of the Gulf Stream, . . . and us on the flying bridge steering in shorts and no tops and at night anchored behind the barrier reef down at Paraiso with the sea pounding on the lovely sand."[13]

On December 21, 1945, he divorced Martha on grounds of desertion. Then he and Mary left for Cuba and were married on March 14, 1946, in Havana. Still hoping for her son's happiness, if not his redemption, his mother wrote from River Forest, Illinois, saying, "I have never lost hope for you, not ceased to pray that the Great Awakening will come to you. Before this life closes . . . What sort of a woman is Mary Welch [sic]?"[14]

By this point in his life, Ernest had lived in many places, but Cuba was where he would live the longest and the place where he seemed the most at home. Mary shared his enthusiasm for hunting, fishing, and spending days at a time aboard the *Pilar*. She gave up her career and became an accomplished cook and hostess. Ernest summarized her virtues for *Look* magazine, saying, "Miss Mary is durable. She is also brave, charming, witty, exciting to look at, a pleasure to be with and a good wife. She is an excellent fisher-woman, a fair wing shot, a strong swimmer, a really good cook, and good judge of wine, and excellent gardener . . . and can run a boat or a household in Spanish."[15]

Running the household at Finca Vigia was no small task. The house and guesthouse were set on fifteen acres that contained flower and vegetable gardens, fruit trees, eighteen different kinds of mangoes, and a variety of trees that supported orchids in addition to a swimming pool and tennis court. The "charming ruin" of the house contained a fifty-foot living room, dining room, library, guest bedroom, and master bedroom as well as a wing that housed a study, bedroom, and bathroom, where Ernest would write. Mary also built a tower as a quiet place where Ernest could work. However, despite, or perhaps because of, the sweeping view of palms leading out to the sea, Ernest preferred to write in his study in the house.

The house was filled with Ernest's favorite things. In addition to comfortable furniture that was designed by Mary and handmade

Jack "Bumby" and Patrick "Mouse" Hemingway reading in the living room at Finca Vigia. *Hemingway Collection, John F. Kennedy Presidential Library and Museum.*

Ernest and Mary Hemingway with Juan "Sinsky" Dunabeitia, Gianfranco Iv-ancich, and others in the dining room at Finca Vigia. *Hemingway Collection, John F. Kennedy Presidential Library and Museum*

in Cuba, the house was populated with horned animal heads in almost every room. The library contained five thousand books, but there also were books in the bedrooms, his study, and his bath-room and a large magazine rack packed with American and foreign magazines and newspapers. Thanks to Mary, the Finca became a comfortable setting for Ernest to write as well as to entertain his friends and family.

Ernest's friends came from a broad range of backgrounds—refugees from the Spanish Civil War, fishermen and boat captains he met on the docks, as well as Hollywood stars who appeared in the film versions of his books. Dinner regulars included Roberto Herrera, who came to Cuba after being imprisoned for fighting on the Loyalist side in the Spanish Civil War; Sinsky Dunabeitia, a Basque boat captain who manned a freighter that ran between the United States and Cuba; and Father Don Andres, whom Ernest called "Black Priest." Like Herrera, Father Don Andres had been involved in the Spanish Civil War, first advising his parishioners to grab their guns and fight rather than spending time in church and then as a machine gunner for the Loyalist army. Kicked out of Spain when the war ended, he came to Cuba but was assigned to a poor parish as the Church took a dim view of his participation in the war. Black Priest, Roberto, and Ernest would eat, drink, swim in the pool, and enjoy hours of reminiscing about their adventures during the Spanish Civil War.

Ernest moored the *Pilar* in the harbor at the village of Cojimar, and his circle of friends was broadened by the local fishermen he met there. His capacity for friendship was enhanced by his broad smile, gregarious nature and his skill at storytelling. From his boyhood days at Walloon Lake until the end of his life, Ernest enjoyed male companionship. In the company of like-minded men, he would relax by telling stories or by fishing, hunting, or just drinking.

The village of Cojimar became the setting for *The Old Man and the Sea*, and it was there on the docks as well as in the bars that Ernest befriended numerous fishermen. They so loved him that at

The statue at Cojimar commissioned by the local fishermen to commemorate the death of Ernest Hemingway. *N. Sindelar Collection*

his death, they melted their boat propellers and anchors to create a bronze statue in his memory. The statue overlooks the harbor and is the most notable piece of architecture in the village.

In 1950 a group of fishermen also proposed to name an international fishing tournament after Ernest out of respect for his passion for fishing and to attract foreign yachtsmen to Cuba. In addition to competing in and giving his name to the Hemingway International Fishing Tournament, Ernest donated the large silver cup that became the tournament trophy, contributed to the creation of the tournament's rules, and presented the trophy to Fidel Castro when he won the competition in 1960.

Ernest's friendships with Spanish refugees and Cuban fishermen were balanced by visits from Hollywood celebrities. Virtually all of Ernest's major novels and short stories were made into movies.

Ernest and Mary Hemingway and Spencer Tracy at the bar at La Floridita, Havana, Cuba, circa 1955. (Left to right: Roberto Herrera, Byra "Puck" Whittlesey, Jack "Bumby" Hemingway, Spencer Tracy, Ernest Hemingway, Mary Hemingway, and an unidentified bartender.) *Hemingway Collection, John F. Kennedy Presidential Library and Museum*

Helen Hayes and Gary Cooper were in the first version of *A Farewell to Arms*, Rock Hudson and Jennifer Jones in the second version. Tyrone Power, Mel Ferrer, Errol Flynn, and Ava Gardner were in *The Sun Also Rises*; Gary Cooper and Ingrid Bergman in *For Whom the Bell Tolls*; and Spencer Tracy in *The Old Man and the Sea*. Burt Lancaster and Ava Gardner starred in "The Killers" and Gregory Peck and Susan Hayward in "The Snows of Kilimanjaro."

In general, Ernest did not like the movie business. It interrupted his morning work schedule and often created unwanted visitors. Nor did he like Hollywood's interpretations of his work. After seeing *The Old Man and the Sea*, he said Spencer Tracy looked like "a fat, very rich actor playing a fisherman."[16] He told Gary Cooper, "Coops the picture business is not for me . . . after the *Old Man and the Sea* . . . I will not ever have anything to do with pictures again so Help Me God."[17]

However, Ernest's ability to make friends, even in Hollywood, remained intact. Gary Cooper became Ernest's Sun Valley hunting companion and slept in his library when he visited the Finca. Ava Gardner became a bullfight aficionada, had a relationship with the celebrated matador Luis Miguel Dominguin, and supposedly swam naked in the pool at Finca Vigia.

In addition to being a favorite retreat of Spanish Civil War refugees, local fishermen, and Hollywood stars, Finca Vigia also became a comfortable and enjoyable destination for visits by Ernest's three boys. Following the paternal values of his own father, Ernest taught his boys to hunt and fish and encouraged their scholarship. He had loved his own father, and his interest in the outdoor life and education were gifts he enjoyed his entire life. Like his father, Ernest passed those gifts along to his sons. Though it appears he tried to avoid having children and was somewhat annoyed by crying babies, his affection for his boys grew as they matured. His letters provide examples of fatherly directives, pride in his sons' accomplishments, and thoughtfully planned adventures to teach them the skills of hunting and fishing.

He gave his children affectionate nicknames: John was Bumby, Patrick was Mouse, and Gregory was Gigi. Trying to coordinate his travels with his children's school vacations so they could be together at the Finca, he told Patrick, "Mousie I rely on you, *no matter how busy*, to see that the Passports are in order and write me the vacation dates. Soon as I know that and when I know my dates can get a cable relayed to Mother. Had hoped to get back for Thanksgiving, but couldn't swing it. Regret very much as we would have had fine time together."[18]

Like his father, Ernest encouraged reading and the foundations of a good education at home. When Bumby first traveled to Key West from Paris, Ernest made certain the boy had a tutor and was learning standard English and then sent regular checks to Hadley as contributions to his education fund. As Bumby matured, he was a good student, and Ernest proudly wrote to Pauline's parents that he was "first in his class and second in the school."[19]

Regular adventures aboard the *Pilar* also contributed to his sons' educations. In January 1936, he wrote a lengthy letter to Pauline's mother describing Patrick's good companionship and interest in fishing despite being seasick.

> It was very rough and his stomach was very upset. I was steering and saw him throwing up over the side and heard him, in the midst of it, shouting "Papa! Papa!" I jumped to him to see what was the matter and he said, "There's a sailfish jumping over there. I just saw him while I was throwing up!"[20]

Ernest went on to say to the approving audience of the boy's grandmother, "He is getting very tough and was very merry about throwing up. . . . I was never a great child lover but these kids are really good company and are very funny and I think (though may be prejudiced) very smart."[21]

Ernest also repeated the pattern of escaping summer heat by vacationing in cooler northern climates. As a child, his family retreated to Walloon Lake. As a parent living in Key West, Ernest regularly took his family to the Nordquists' L-Bar T Ranch in the Big Horn Mountains of Wyoming to escape the heat and hurricanes of Key West. While Ernest maintained his practice of writing in the mornings, in the afternoons he and his boys would fish for trout or hunt for deer, elk, or bear.

While the boys lived with their natural mothers after the divorces of their parents, Ernest seems to have chosen new wives that welcomed and nurtured his sons. Though Pauline engaged a staff of nursemaids and nannies to raise the children, she accepted Bumby as her own. She even persuaded Uncle Gus to establish a trust fund for him as well as endowing Patrick and Gregory. Though Martha spent less time with the boys, they hunted together in Wyoming, and the boys were impressed with her independent spirit and her ability to punctuate sentences with four-letter words. Martha developed genuine affection for Ernest's sons, especially fifteen-year-old Bumby. At one point Martha wrote to Hadley and said that she didn't "see how a woman could produce a better or more beautiful boy."[22]

By the time Ernest married Mary Welsh, the boys certainly were used to change in their father's partners and continued to enjoy the comforts of life at Finca Vigia as well as the excitement of the Gulf Stream. Patrick remembered the Finca as

> some of the loveliest land I've seen. Mango trees lined the driveway leading up to the house, and tall royal palms grew beside the path leading down to the swimming pool in back. Flower and bougainvillea vines bloomed all over. Hummingbirds made their tiny neat square nests in the tropical foliage.[23]

Though there were periods of friction between Ernest and his sons, especially Gregory, all embraced their father's love of the outdoors and valued education. Bumby (Jack) attended the University of Montana and Dartmouth College and then enlisted in the U.S. Army after the attack on Pearl Harbor. As a French-speaking first lieutenant in the Office of Strategic Services (OSS), the U.S. wartime intelligence agency, he parachuted into occupied France with his fly rod, reel, and flies. Though he escaped being captured on that mission, in late October 1944 he was wounded and captured by the Germans and held prisoner of war at Mosberg Prison Camp until April 1945. Throughout his life, Jack Hemingway was an avid fly fisherman and published an autobiography, *Misadventures of a Fly Fisherman: My Life With and Without Papa.*

Patrick graduated from Harvard and then moved to East Africa where he was a professional big game hunter and safari operator. After his return to the United States, he settled in Montana.

Gregory attended St. John's College in Annapolis, Maryland, and eventually received a medical degree. He practiced medicine first in New York and then as a rural family doctor in Montana.

Ernest Hemingway and sons Patrick "Mouse" and Jack "Bumby" with a freshly caught tuna. Bimini, Bahamas, circa 1930s. *Hemingway Collection, John F. Kennedy Presidential Library and Museum*

Ernest Hemingway with sons Patrick "Mouse," Jack "Bumby," and Gregory "Gigi" after pigeon shooting at Club de Cazadores, Cuba, circa 1945. *Hemingway Collection, John F. Kennedy Presidential Library and Museum*

Though clearly there were major conflicts between the boys and their father, Gregory summarized their feelings for their father by saying, "Although we always called him Papa, it was out of love not fear."[24]

The years Ernest and Mary spent together at the Finca were punctuated with numerous requests for biographical interviews. Of great interest to biographical interviewers were Ernest's patrol activities aboard the *Pilar* and his intelligence activities at Rambouillet. Given Ernest's love of storytelling, he sometimes said too much about what still was secret information. He later regretted telling interviewers that he operated as a counterintelligence agent while pretending to be fishing. He feared that he would be in trouble with the Cuban government if his pro-American wartime activities became public information. Ironically, when he did return to the United States, he thought he was constantly being watched by the FBI due to his pro-American intelligence activities while in Cuba.

The solitude of Finca Vigia also was interrupted by requests for written work and movie rights. Ernest exchanged numerous letters with Pete Viertel, who wrote the screenplays for *The Sun Also Rises* and *The Old Man and the Sea*. They considered projects that included making a documentary with John Huston about Cuban revolutionists and collaborating on a novel that involved the crew of a disabled German submarine taking over the Cayo Lobos lighthouse and being discovered by men aboard the *Pilar*. Ernest wanted to write the *Pilar* side of the story and thought Viertel should research and write the German side.

Both projects eventually stalled, but their letters provide insight into Ernest's business sense. Clearly, he liked discussing and planning the projects, but in almost every letter he digresses from the details of the projects to planning hunting and fishing trips. He tells Viertel,

> If Huston comes down here get the hell down with him. I'll have to work all Spring and summer but I don't work afternoons and we could get out in the boat a couple of time[s] a week anyway. I don't think there is any chance to get out West but we will see you gusys [sic] surely in the fall. I'll let you know as soon as I hear that bird seasons are set.[25]

While he didn't work effectively on collaborative projects, Ernest also had mixed emotions about returning to "the movie business." He never was satisfied with the film versions of his novels and short stories. However, the $12,000 he received for the film rights to "The Snows of Kilimanjaro" funded his much anticipated return to Italy.

Ernest and Mary returned to Italy in October 1948. They planned to spend the fall in Venice and the winter in Cortina d'Ampezzo. During the fall Ernest hunted for ducks and Mary visited museums. When Mary left Venice to prepare the rented house in Cortina, Ernest hunted at Baron Nanyuki Franchetti's lodge north of Venice. There he met the Ivancich family and became absolutely captivated by their eighteen-year-old daughter, Adriana. He saw her every day during the 1948 visit to Venice, lunching at the Gritti Palace Hotel, drinking at Harry's Bar, and strolling along the canals of Venice. After Mary broke her ankle skiing in Cortina, and Ernest contracted an eye infection that sent him to the hospital in Padua for ten days, they returned to the Finca.

After intense correspondence, Adriana, her brother Gianfranco, and her mother, who acted as a chaperon, visited Finca Vigia in 1950. Ernest continued to be infatuated with Adriana and during her visit behaved erratically and emotionally. He tried to precipitate a break with Mary, but despite his embarrassing and humiliating actions and comments, Mary stayed the course, saying, "No matter what you say or do . . . I'm going to stay here and run your house and your Finca."[26]

Again writing from his personal experience, Ernest used Adriana as the model for Renata in *Across the River and into the Trees.* Renata, like Adriana, was from an aristocratic Venetian family and had lost both her father and her ancestral villa to the violence of World War II. The plot of the novel centers on the comfort and renewal the fifty-year-old Colonel Cantwell finds in his love for the nineteen-year-old Renata and his determination to experience her love of life and youthful sense of immortality until the very end.

In reality, everyone except Ernest saw Ernest's infatuation with Adriana as an embarrassing midlife folly of an aging writer. Though Adriana was attracted to Ernest because she believed she could restore energy to his writing, she did not feel the same intensity of

Ernest and Mary Hemingway outside the Gritti Palace Hotel in Venice circa 1948. *Hemingway Collection, John F. Kennedy Presidential Library and Museum*

Ernest and Mary Hemingway with Adriana Ivancich and others at La Floridita in Havana, Cuba, circa 1950. (Left to right: Roberto Hererra, unidentified man, Gianfranco Ivancich, Mary Hemingway, Dora Ivancich, Ernest Hemingway, and Adriana Ivancich.) *Hemingway Collection, John F. Kennedy Presidential Library and Museum*

affection as he did. He once told her, "I would ask you to marry me if I didn't know you would say 'no.'"[27] She later said, "I appreciated his kindnesses and his attention. We were friends."[28]

Despite the intensity of emotion Ernest felt for Adriana and the energy he put into writing the novel, the formula of love and war that had been so successful in *A Farewell to Arms* and *For Whom the Bell Tolls* did not work in *Across the River and into the Trees*. While Cantwell's affair with Renata is clearly drawn from Ernest's infatuation with Adriana, their "love story" is as improbable and unrealistic to the reader as Ernest's May-September love for Adriana was to his wife and friends.

No one but Ernest approved of the book. Mary found the conversations between Colonel Cantwell and his girl "banal beyond reason."[29] Adriana, who attended a Catholic girls' school and was well trained in aristocratic Venetian values, believed, "A girl like that does not exist, if she is lovely and from a good family and goes to Mass every morning. Such a girl would not drink all day like a sponge and be in bed at the hotel."[30] The critics agreed. Maxwell Geismar said in the *Saturday Review of Literature* that not only was *Across the River and into the Trees* Ernest's "worst novel," but "a synthesis of everything that is bad in his previous work."[31]

The parallels between Ernest's lifelong interest in hunting and his quest for the youthful Adriana also were not lost on the critics. Many believed that the bases of his pleasures when hunting were the rituals and the satisfaction associated with conquest, and that to some extent Ernest's relationships with women were based on the same needs and his desire to collect trophies.[32]

Ernest's interlude with Adriana was consistent with his pattern of escaping the routine of married life. No matter how good his life was with Hadley or Pauline, he left for a new adventure. The difference in the situation with Adriana was she was not interested in Ernest as a romantic partner, and Mary refused to leave him despite his behavior. After Adriana and her mother left Finca Vigia, her brother Gianfranco remained. Ernest seemed to find the young man's friendship a consolation for the missing Adriana. Gianfranco had the war and bravery credentials Hemingway could respect. He was wounded in the North African campaign of World War II and had discovered his father's body after being murdered, presumably by Fascists.

With Adriana's departure, Ernest settled down and focused on rescuing his reputation as a writer. He had defended *Across the River and into the Trees* saying,

> Sure, they can say anything about nothing happening in *Across the River*, but all that happens is the defense of the lower Piave, the breakthrough in Normandy, the taking of Paris and the destruction of the 22nd Infantry in Hurtgen Forest plus a man who loves a girl and dies.[33]

However, he knew he had to reply to the critics who had said he was through as a writer.

Because Ernest had used specific personal experiences as the content for many successful short stories and novels, his critics claimed he could write about nothing except himself and his own experiences. Assuming the criticism was valid, Ernest began developing a character that was not as personally connected with himself as Frederic Henry, Robert Jordan, and Colonel Cantwell had been. The character was an old fisherman, one he knew from the harbor at Cojimar. Alone in a skiff, the old man catches a great marlin, only to have it destroyed by sharks. While the old man's loss was not personally experienced by Ernest, the character's unsuccessful efforts to bring in the marlin reflect Ernest's own unsuccessful experiences with the politely indifferent Adriana and the unsuccessful reception to *Across the River and into the Trees*. Like the old man, Ernest may have dared to venture too far from the shore on the wide blue Gulf Stream of life and been attacked by sharklike critics. Like the old man, who had been a champion arm wrestler and a successful fisherman, Ernest too was trying for a comeback.

Though Ernest was not the old man, his fishing experiences did contribute to the book. He knew well the inhabitants of the Gulf Stream and the pattern of one, then two, then more sharks attacking a valuable catch as well as the sensation of killing a shark by driving a knife blade between its vertebrae and brain. He knew too the details of the old man's skiff and what he would have had on board and the order he would use the items to counter the attack of sharks—first, a harpoon; then, a knife lashed to the butt of an oar; and finally the tiller and rudder. He made use of his twenty years' experience on the Gulf: "[He] knew about a man in that situation with a fish. [He] knew what happened in a boat, in a sea, fighting a fish. So [he] took a man [he] knew for twenty years and imagined him under those circumstances."[34]

The old man also embraces the code for living that Ernest first developed based on his experiences in World War I—the experiences in which a man confronts an unconquerable element. This time it wasn't man confronting the circumstances of war and almost certain death, but man confronting sharks and almost certain death. The old man exhibits courage and grace under pressure. He fights the sharks, believing "a man can be destroyed, but not defeated."[35]

The reviews and success of the book were nothing less than phenomenal. The *New Republic* called Ernest "unquestionably the greatest craftsman in the American novel in this century."[36] The *New York Times* claimed, "Here is the master technician once more at the top of his form, doing superbly what he can do better than anyone else."[37] Appropriately, Ernest was aboard the *Pilar* and out on the Gulf Stream when he heard via the ship's radio that the book had been awarded the Pulitzer Prize. Advance sales of the Scribner's publication ran to fifty thousand with more weekly sales of three thousand copies thereafter. Because of the simplicity of style and the universality of its theme, the book was translated into numerous languages. In addition to U.S. and foreign royalties, Ernest sold the film rights for $150,000.

Having regained his reputation as the greatest craftsman of the American novel, Ernest and Mary headed back to Franco's Spain for bullfights in Pamplona and then to Africa to visit Patrick and engage in another safari. Unfortunately, the trips were disappointing and began what would be a series of events that would precipitate the decline of a great writer.

Ernest and Mary Hemingway on safari in Africa, circa 1954. *Hemingway Collection, John F. Kennedy Presidential Library and Museum.*

Wreckage of the Cessna 180 plane that carried Ernest and Mary Hemingway while on their African safari, near Murchison Falls, Uganda, January 1954. *Hemingway Collection, John F. Kennedy Presidential Library and Museum*

Ernest found Pamplona crowded and the bullfights disappointing; Mary was bothered by the dry climate and the noise. As a result, they spent more time than usual in the Prado. When they left Spain, they boarded a ship in Marseilles and headed to Mombasa to begin the second half of what Ernest would eventually call his "chicken-shit" crusade. Ernest, Mary, and their entourage and guide began the safari south of Nairobi, enjoying the scenery and the opportunity to hunt for leopards.

As a gift to Mary, Ernest chartered a small Cessna 180 for the purpose of sightseeing in the Belgian Congo. After seeing herds of hippopotamus, elephants, and buffalo, and flying over Murchison Falls, they were heading back to Entebbe when the plane encountered a large flock of birds. Trying to avoid a collision, the pilot struck a telegraph wire and the plane crashed into low trees and heavy brush. Though Mary, Ernest, and the pilot all were injured, they survived the crash. After spending the night above a crocodile-infested river, they sighted a boat and were able to take it to Butiaba. There they boarded a De Havilland Rapide, hoping to head back to Entebbe, where reporters were waiting to learn whether the rumors that Ernest had been killed were true.

Shortly after takeoff the De Havilland Rapide crashed and began to burn. Mary and the pilot escaped by kicking out a window. Ernest tried to escape through a door, but it turned out to be jammed. As the cabin burned, he used his dislocated shoulder and head to finally open the door and exited onto the lower left wing of the biplane. When fully examined, he learned he not only had a dislocated shoulder, but also had another concussion, two cracked discs in his spine, and ruptures in his liver and one of his kidneys.

After their return to the Finca, Ernest's moods became increasingly irritable. He ached from his injuries and was besieged by guests, curious tourists, and movie people. In addition to the physical irritations, he saw the signs of revolution brewing in Cuba. The Batista regime was being challenged by Fidel Castro. Ernest did not support Batista and hoped that Castro would just leave him alone, but the pressure to leave Cuba mounted when the Castro regime began vilifying the United States. Then one night a Batista search party tried to enter the Finca, looking for guns. One of the soldiers clubbed to death Ernest's favorite Black Dog, using the butt of his rifle. Knowing the atrocities that occurred on both sides during the Spanish Civil War, Ernest decided it was time to purchase a house in Idaho.

Again Ernest's predictions were correct. Batista's officials were arrested and trials of his soldiers ended in executions. The American press was enraged, and Castro decided to go to the United States to refute claims about his leadership. When Ernest heard about Castro's decision to visit the States, he contacted him in order to give him his thoughts about what to expect. During their meeting, they discussed the biases of various U.S. publications, the likelihood that Castro would be heckled, and the need for direct answers about Communism. When Castro was questioned on the *This Is Your Life* television program, he began his answer with "Let me tell you what Ernest Hemingway thinks about that: The executions in Cuba are a necessary phenomena. The military criminals who were executed by the revolutionary government received what they deserved."[38] When U.S. reporters heard the news that Batista had fled Cuba and Castro had taken over the country, they immediately contacted Ernest on New Year's Day, 1959. He told them that he was "delighted," though he later changed the word to "hopeful."[39]

Given the tense political climate in Cuba, Ernest jumped at the opportunity to go to Spain when he was invited there to join his Idaho friend, Bill Davis. Their plan was to witness a *mano a mano*, a bullfight in which two matadors alternate, competing for the admiration of the audience. In addition to witnessing an extraordinary contest between Antonio Ordonez and Luis Miguel Dominguin, *Life* contacted Ernest to write an article on the new season of bullfighting.

Ernest dedicated himself to the article. After witnessing the *mano a mano*, he returned to Cuba in November 1959. Upon his return he expressed support of the Castro regime by kissing the Cuban flag, and in May 1960 presented Castro with the silver cup for winning the Hemingway Fishing Tournament. Then that summer he went back to Spain to check facts and collect photographs. He worked feverishly on the article, now titled "Dangerous Summer," which was exceeding the word count of the original contract.

While in Spain he wrote to Mary. His letters were foreboding: "Only thing I am afraid of, no not only thing, is complete physical and nervous crack-up from deadly over work";[40] "I wish you were here to look after me and help me out and keep [me] from cracking up."[41] He was becoming the victim of the complications and demands that resulted from his own legendary lifestyle and remarkable career as a writer.

During the early Paris years he had received numerous rejection letters, but worked hard, wrote well, and loved only Hadley. Now he had the responsibilities associated with three ex-wives and three children and constantly was being pressured for his stories and advice. He owned property around the world, felt responsible for the education and well-being of his boys, and had to make up for sarcastic comments and sidebar flirtations with younger women by giving Mary fur coats and diamond brooches.

Though once forced to cut words or stories to meet the censorship demands of his publishers, now he had no problems with extensions in deadlines, changes in word count, or even vocabulary. *Life* wanted his bullfighting article whenever it came. Scribner's knew a new Hemingway book would make their year—and were eager to publish his Paris memoirs. In addition, he and A. E. Hotchner had formed a lucrative partnership that developed television programming based on his short stories and novels. Four shows would bring them $240,000, and more shows were requested. Unlike the early years, he was making a lot of money—for himself, his publishers, and his producers. However, his body was deteriorating and his moods were increasingly irrational.

Chapter Six

The Departure to
Sun Valley

"Is dying hard, Daddy?"
"No, I think it's pretty easy, Nick. It all depends."

—"Indian Camp," Ernest Hemingway, 1925[1]

Ernest and Mary Hemingway outside the Sun Valley Lodge, circa 1947.
Hemingway Collection, John F. Kennedy Presidential Library and Museum

ERNEST WAS FIRST INTRODUCED TO SUN VALLEY, IDAHO, in 1939
when Averell Harriman developed the resort as a destination for
travelers on his Union Pacific Railroad. Ernest was invited to stay
at the Sun Valley Lodge as a guest. Gene Vann Guilder, the resort
publicist, thought the now famous author and outdoorsman would
enjoy the mountains of Idaho and might generate some good publicity for the resort. At Sun Valley Ernest joined Gary Cooper, Bar-
bara Stanwyck, Ingrid Bergman, and other celebrities who also were
offered free accommodations in an effort to promote the resort.
Attracted to the ambiance of the now famous Sun Valley Lodge,
the beauty of the Sawtooth Mountains, and the abundance of wild
game, Ernest often returned to Sun Valley for duck hunting.

Ernest made friends with the local ranchers, but also interacted
with a sophisticated and wealthy group of friends who were drawn
to the isolation of the rugged mountain setting. He especially enjoyed hunting with Gary Cooper, who had played the role of Robert Jordan in *For Whom the Bell Tolls*, and balanced his hunting

Ernest Hemingway and Gary Cooper after hunting in Sun Valley, circa 1959.
Hemingway Collection, John F. Kennedy Presidential Library and Museum

and fishing expeditions with dinners at the Sun Valley Lodge, the Christiana Inn, and Trail Creek Cabin. In 1959 he told Gianfranco Ivancich, "Very nice people live here in these valleys. The farmers and ranchers. We shoot together and have fun. Mary made a party for 40 people two days after Christmas at Trail Creek Cabin and it was very good."[2]

When Ernest first visited Sun Valley, he had a reputation for being indestructible. His larger-than-life legend was built not only on the strength and courage of the heroes in his novels and short stories, but also on his personal life. Photographs of the author on African safaris, deep-sea fishing aboard the *Pilar*, and attending bullfights in Spain, as well as his frontline involvement in World War I, the Spanish Civil War, and World War II all contributed to the image of the adventurous, masculine author. Coupled with his handsome smile and his ability to charm listeners with storytelling, a legendary figure was created and admired around the world and in Sun Valley.

Though Ernest associated with and charmed the celebrities that were drawn to the resort, he still maintained a strong need for privacy. His original motivation for going to Sun Valley was for hunting and fishing, not to mingle with movie stars. When restrictions were placed on hunting and his name was used to attract visitors, he didn't like it. Writing to Pete Viertel in 1948, he said,

> This to explain how [I] feel at the moment about Idaho. I love it but lots of times last fall, after hunting was over, I felt like it was time to pull out for a new country. You know that when they are having pictures painted of you and hung in real estate promotion offices it is past time to blow. Do not want to be an elder statesman nor a credit to the community nor a[n] asset; want to start over as a mountain man and open up a new country and get the hell out when the game begins to think or if they incorporate the town.[3]

Later that year he wrote from Venice, saying, "I had a hunch I was through with S.V. last year [with the] 4 duck limit, closing [of] gambling, wholesale appearance of jerks, conventions etc. Lovely place but there is always another frontier even if you have to go in reverse to find it. . . . Here you can shoot 100 ducks if you can shoot well enough."[4]

Ernest and Mary Hemingway's house in Ketchum, Idaho. *Caroline Clawson, Idaho Nature Conservancy*

Despite his reservations about being a celebrity in Sun Valley, he decided the resort would be a safe haven when political conditions began to deteriorate in Cuba. After years of either staying at the Sun Valley Lodge or renting a cabin, Ernest bought a house near Sun Valley in April 1959. Based on his experiences in the Spanish Civil War, he knew the consequences of a revolution or a civil war. He told Patrick,

> Cuba is really bad now, Mouse. I am not a big fear danger pussy but living in a country where no one is right—both sides atrocious—knowing what sort of stuff and murder will go on when the new ones come in—seeing the abuses of those in now—I am fed on it. We are always treated OK as in all countries and have fine good friends. But things aren't good. . . . Might pull out.[5]

When Ernest and Mary decided to "pull out" of Cuba, they moved to a house about a mile from the Sun Valley resort in the town of Ketchum. The square, rather fortresslike house was built on a hillside overlooking the Big Wood River and had large picture windows from which to view the majestic Sawtooth Mountains. Set on seventeen acres of aspens and cottonwood trees, the location offered privacy and the back bedroom was identified as an ideal study for Ernest. The refuge was purchased from the millionaire sportsman, Bob Topping, for $50,000.

By the time Ernest actually lived in the house, his ailments from various injuries; the pressures for more articles, short stories, and novels; and the political complications of being a U.S. citizen with a house in Cuba began to take their toll. In his desire to fully live a courageous life of action, Ernest suffered numerous injuries. In addition to two skull fractures and at least seven other concussions and other subconcussive head traumas, he developed an enlarged liver due to heavy use of alcohol and skin cancer due to many hours in the sun, as well as back problems that now prevented him from skiing.

By 1960 the injuries and ailments affected not only his physical health but also his mental health. He became increasingly moody and irrational, and writing was a struggle. After numerous trips to Spain to write "Dangerous Summer" for *Life*, he had exceeded the number of words specified in his contract. The original contract was for ten thousand words, but the manuscript had grown to 120,000 words. Ernest spent months agonizing over how to edit it, but couldn't let go of the details that he felt were so important to the total effect of the story. Given his struggle, cuts eventually were made to create a forty-thousand-word article by the managing editor of *Life*, and Scribner's agreed to do a full-length book version of 130,000 words, also called *The Dangerous Summer*.

Prior to leaving Cuba, Ernest also had been working on what he called his Paris book. Much to his pleasure, a trunk filled with notebooks and writing from his Paris years had been discovered at the Paris Ritz. In 1957, while still in Cuba, Ernest began to use his notes to craft a memoir. Though he wrote with enthusiasm while in Cuba, when he tried to write the concluding paragraphs two years later in Sun Valley, he just couldn't do it. The Paris book, which became *A Moveable Feast*, had to be published posthumously without the final paragraphs he tried so hard to write.

Ernest Hemingway at home in Ketchum, Idaho, circa 1960. *Hemingway Collection, John F. Kennedy Presidential Library and Museum*

In 1960 Ernest and Mary were invited to President Kennedy's 1961 inauguration, but declined on the grounds of Ernest's poor health. When asked to compose a simple message for a presentation volume for the new president, Ernest again was tormented by writer's block. With much effort, he finally wrote,

> Watching the inauguration from Rochester there was the happiness and the hope and the pride and how beautiful we thought Mrs. Kennedy was and how deeply moving the inaugural address was. Watching on the [TV] screen I was sure our President would stand any of the heat to come as he had taken the cold of that day. Each day since I have renewed my faith and tried to understand the practical difficulties of governing he must face as they arise and admire the true courage he brings to them. It is a good thing to have a brave man as our President in times as tough as these are for our country and the world.[6]

Though Ernest's words still reflect his lifelong focus on grace under pressure and his interest in a man's courage and bravery in "times as tough as these," his mental and physical decline is easily

Ernest Hemingway at home in Ketchum, Idaho, circa 1960. *Hemingway Collection, John F. Kennedy Presidential Library and Museum*

measured by his struggle in writing the brief message to the new president and his willingness to reject the opportunity to attend the inauguration as a guest of honor and passively watch it on television.

Throughout his life, writing had been Ernest's major source of pleasure and the basis for his self-esteem and self-confidence. He worked to make his writing clear and concise and organized his days to write in the mornings and play in the afternoons. He set goals for the number of pages to be written daily, kept careful track of the number of pages he wrote, and was happiest when he was being productive as a writer. Often he wrote to his editor and friend Max Perkins to report on the progress of his work. From Key West he had summarized his progress on *A Farewell to Arms*, saying, "Have 20 chapters done and typed—must be around 30,000 words—have been over the whole thing once in pencil and re-read it all. Going good but have been working 6–10 hours every day and will be glad to layoff and take a trip when you come down."[7] When writing became difficult, his daily routine was destroyed along with his self-confidence. Ernest's creativity was replaced by anxiety.

In addition to the anxiety created by not being able to write, Ernest believed he was being followed by the FBI. He was suspicious of strangers in restaurants and males in topcoats. Though his paranoia was taking control of his life, his suspicions were not unfounded. Whether he knew it or not, the FBI had opened a file on him at the time of his 1940s Crook Factory operation in Cuba, and the local Havana agent reported regularly on his activities for the rest of his life.

Ernest had initiated what he called the "Crook Factory" as a counterintelligence unit to report on pro-Nazi Falangist sympathizers in Cuba during World War II. Though outlawed by the Cuban government, the pro-Nazi Falange was active and dangerous to American interests because of its ability to aid Nazi initiatives. Ernest and the American ambassador to Cuba were concerned about the loyalties of Spanish residents in Cuba as well as the possibility of Franco's Spain joining the Axis powers. With the approval of the American ambassador, Ernest recruited Spanish exiles from the anti-Franco Loyalist cause and local Cubans he met in bars and restaurants to gather information on Falangist activities. Their Crook Factory "headquarters" were in his guesthouse at the Finca.

Initially Ernest's Crook Factory reports were considered valued information and were sent unedited to the U.S. State Department. U.S. ambassador to Cuba Spruille Braden said Ernest "built up an excellent organization and did an A-one job."[8] However, Ernest's support of the Loyalist cause during the Spanish Civil War and his recruitment of Spanish exiles from the Loyalist cause gave rise to questions about the extent to which Ernest supported Communism. After all, the Loyalists in Spain had been supported by the Russian Communists.

In 1942 D. M. Ladd wrote to J. Edgar Hoover, director of the FBI, in Washington, D.C., saying, "Hemingway has been accused of being of Communist sympathy, although we are advised that he has denied and does vigorously deny any Communist affiliation or sympathy."[9] The same letter went on to comment on the "extreme danger of having some informant like Hemingway given free rein to stir up trouble such as which will undoubtedly ensue if this situation continues . . . and that Hemingway's services as an informant will be discontinued."[10]

Though Ernest did not embrace Communism, he did not like Batista and believed "he looted [Cuba] naked when he left."[11] When Ernest returned to Cuba from Spain in 1959, he expressed his support for Castro to reporters, saying, "I am very happy to be here again because I consider myself a Cuban. I have not believed any of the reports against Cuba. I sympathize with the Cuban government and with all our difficulties."[12] When he kissed the hem of the Cuban flag, the event was also recorded in his FBI file.

Ernest's paranoia about being followed by the FBI and his frustration over his inability to write were further complicated by his worries about his financial situation. After World War II he had worked himself into a postwar tax bracket of 90 percent. Despite a steady stream of income of royalties from around the world, solid investments in stock, and a valuable art collection, he was concerned about his ability to pay his income tax as well as property taxes on houses in Florida, Idaho, and Cuba and land in Ketchum and Bimini. He complained to Mary that she was spending too much on groceries, and his correspondence to friends and his reflections in *A Movable Feast* are testimony to that fact that during this period of financial responsibility and worry, he recalled with fondness the simpler, more frugal life he and Hadley had shared in Paris.

Though he was experiencing the classic signs of depression— loss of self-esteem, a sense of guilt, and periods of agitation and anxiety, Ernest had coped with periods of depression his entire life. He had witnessed his father's depression and suicide, and his letters provide numerous examples that he often put off writing to friends when he was feeling down. In a 1936 letter to Pauline's mother, he apologizes for not writing sooner, saying,

> Had a spell when I was pretty gloomy, that was why I didn't write first, and didn't sleep for about three weeks. Took to getting up about two or so in the morning and going out to the little house to work until daylight because when you're writing on a book and can't sleep your brain races at night and you write all the stuff in your head and in the morning it's gone and you are pooped.[13]

When his local doctor suggested psychiatric treatment, he expressed the typical midwestern reluctance regarding psychiatric help. Concerned about negative publicity, he said, "They'll say I'm losing my marbles."[14] Eventually, however, he registered at the Mayo Clinic in Rochester, Minnesota, under an assumed name. The doctors took him off his blood pressure medicine, which they believed caused depression, and recommended electric shock therapy twice a week to alleviate his depression.

A number of medical professionals and scholars believe that the electric shock treatment he received at the Mayo Clinic actually increased his depression because it further decreased his ability to remember events. The electroconvulsive therapy induced grand mal seizures, which were the equivalent of more concussions. As a result, his memories and experiences were lost, and he felt a sense of despair and futility when he could only vaguely sense the past.

Since personal experience was the source for the content of his writing, this further loss of memory was a catastrophic event. His success as a writer had been built on his keen observation of people, places, and events. He had used his ability to quickly evaluate acquaintances who could help his career as a writer and sometimes even befriended people he didn't really like simply to increase his experiential base for his writing. To facilitate relationships he would alternate acting as a child, hoping people, such as his wives, would care for him, and acting as the parent by offering advice or experience often through his well-crafted gift of storytelling.

His early training in journalism also made him a keen observer of places and events, and he practiced writing and rewriting disciplined descriptions in the economic language that became his trademark. His memories of places, people, and events were the substance of his writing and his success as a writer. Now those memories were gone.

One can only wonder if Ernest wasn't foreshadowing his own decline in *Across the River and into the Trees* and *The Old Man and the Sea*. After he left Oak Park, he became a citizen of the world always exploring new places, new adventures, and new conquests. But when he returned later in life to the places of his earlier adventures, he was disappointed. The juxtaposition of youthful memories and approaching age is explored in his later novels, especially *Across the River and into the Trees* and *The Old Man and the Sea*.

In *Across the River and into the Trees*, the aging Colonel Cantwell tries to recapture his youth by loving a younger woman and by returning to the places of his youth before he dies. Similarly, in *The Old Man and the Sea*, Santiago attempts to revisit the strength and success of his youth and attempts to win something he has lost, but returns home only to dream of lions. Both characters had experienced success and virility in their younger days. Age became their fatal flaw and the source of their personal tragedy.

When Ernest tried to double back on the adventures of his early life, he was disappointed. His letters from Paris after victory against the Germans are filled with a sad nostalgia about the early days with Hadley. Then, after a period of contentment at Finca Vigia, his trips to Spain and Africa also were tainted with disappointment. For a variety of reasons, the festival of San Fermin and the *mano a mano* paled in comparison to the experiences of Ernest the young aficionado. Finally, the much anticipated return to Africa for a second safari resulted in two plane crashes and another concussion. In a stoic letter to Harvey Breit, he said, the second plane crash was "a little bit bad. . . . I ruptured the kidneys, or maybe only one, the liver, the spleen, had the brain fluid ooze out to soak the pillow every night, burnt the top of the scalp off, etc."[15]

Despite the injuries and his "chicken-shit crusades" to places of the past, Ernest still believed in the code of action and ritual that he developed as a result of his experiences in World War I and the importance of facing death with grace and courage. As E. M. Halliday has noted, Ernest consistently reminded his readers as well as himself that "we are part of a universe offering no assurance beyond the grave, and we are to make what we can of life by a pragmatic ethic spun bravely out of man himself in full and steady cognizance that the end is darkness."[16]

Ernest was now at the point where he had made what he could out of his life and personally had to face that the end was darkness. In many ways the boy from Oak Park had become the embodiment of the American Dream. With talent, hard work, ambition, and perseverance, he defined a new set of values and a code for living in the post–World War I world and developed an economy of language in his style of writing that was embraced and translated around the world. In addition to garnering every prize available to a writer, he married women who adored him, fathered handsome children, owned multiple houses in exotic settings, accumulated a valuable art collection, and engaged in daring adventures that captivated a worldwide audience. He had succeeded his dreams and more than fulfilled his high school classmates' prophecy that "none are to be found more clever than Ernie."

Yet, despite, or perhaps because of, his success, he no longer was able to meet his own high expectations. His return visits to places of past excitement and success were disappointing, and the numerous concussions, the paranoia about the FBI, and the undue worry over finances resulted in a state of confusion that limited his ability to write the clear, honest prose that he and his readers had come to expect. He longed for the simpler times. After writing to his old friend Bill Horne about recent kidnappings in Cuba, he added the postscript, "God I wish we were heading out west together again the way we did the year when we first met Bunny."[17] Clearly Ernest was reflecting back on the early support and understanding that Bill's friendship had provided and the adventures they had shared together. Bill too had been a volunteer for the Red Cross in Italy and had witnessed Ernest's injury, recovery, and love for Agnes. When they both returned to the Midwest after the war, Bill offered Ernest modest financial support, was his roommate in a Chicago apartment, participated as a groomsman in his marriage to Hadley, and was a lifelong friend and hunting companion. Unlike Ernest, Bill led a quiet, more conservative life in the United States and was married to the same woman, Bunny, for more than forty years.

In 1954 Ernest told George Plimpton, "Once writing has become your major vice and greatest pleasure only death can stop it."[18] Given his interest in language and in turning phrases, one wonders if he didn't think, "Once one can no longer write, death is the only alternative." He knew "all stories, if continued far enough, end in death,"[19] and had spent most of his life studying death and how man faced it.

During his childhood and adolescence in Oak Park, Ernest's father and grandfathers had introduced him to the ways men confront death. His grandfathers focused on war and the importance of courage and honor. His father's observations were more medical, more scientific and were supported with vivid artifacts such as the dead fetus in a jar in his office or the human skeleton in his closet.

As a Red Cross volunteer, Ernest observed firsthand the bloody results of the bombing of the ammunitions factory in Milan and then faced his own brush with death in the Italian trenches. Then he became fascinated with matadors and used their sense of courage and honor in facing death as an antidote to the dissipation of the lost generation he had encountered in post–World War I Paris. As time passed, a consistent code of behavior was applied to his heroes. All displayed "grace under pressure" when facing death in their roles as soldiers, hunters, and eventually even as an old Cuban fisherman.

Given his preoccupation with the eventuality of death and how man faced it, Ernest had already considered his own end. He believed suicide was a commonsense way for many people to end their lives. He frequently told others exactly how he would execute his own suicide, once saying to Martha that one could place the barrel of a shotgun on one's head and discharge a full blast through the barrel by placing one's toe on the trigger and bearing down.

By the time Ernest moved to Ketchum, he also had observed how many of his friends had died. At first the loss of friends and mentors did not bother him. When Ford Madox Ford, his early boss at the *Transatlantic Review*, died in 1939, Ernest jokingly observed, "People are dying this year that never died before."[20] Then F. Scott Fitzgerald died of a heart attack in Hollywood in 1940, and in 1941 Sherwood Anderson and James Joyce died of peritonitis, and Virginia Woolf, fearing a mental breakdown, put heavy rocks into her pockets and walked into the River Ouse. In 1946 Gertrude Stein died following an operation for cancer, and in 1947 Max Perkins, weakened by pleurisy and pneumonia, died of a heart attack. After Perkins's death no jovial comments were made. Rather, Ernest said, "When Max died I did not think I could stand it. We understood each other so well that it was like having a part of yourself die."[21]

When his mother died in a Memphis hospital in June 1951, she was incapacitated by age and unable to recognize the names or faces of her children. Though she never knew about or was able to appreciate the high honors her son would receive for his writing, she seldom praised his work or offered the recognition he so desired from her. Yet Ernest remembered the importance of her life, "how beautiful she was when she was young," and "how happy we were as children" by arranging to have the church bells ring in San Francisco de Paula the morning of her funeral.[22] Later that year Pauline died the morning after she and Ernest had had a bitter fight about Gregory's drug problems, and in May 1961 Gary Cooper succumbed to cancer.

Though Ernest's ability to make new friends survived his move to Sun Valley, his desire to be with people waned. He became moody and depressed and wanted to be alone. However, despite his mood swings and frequent verbal attacks, Mary honored the commitment that she understood would be necessary when they first courted in Paris. She continued to accept the fact that Ernest wanted, and now needed, a "practical nurse." As she witnessed his decline, she believed his personality changed. She said he was "almost the opposite of what he had been before—outgoing and exuberant and articulate and full of life." Now he was "all inward and quiet and inarticulate."[23]

In 1945 when Ernest told Malcolm Crowley that "writing is a very lonely trade,"[24] he was experienced in balancing his loneliness by attracting and befriending a broad range of people. Some were rich, others poor. Some educated, others not. Many became the bases for characters in his novels and short stories. Others were writers and editors who became mentors, critics, loyal supporters, and rivals as well as friends.

Ernest's ability to make friends and enjoy companionship was a lifelong pattern first established during the summers at Walloon Lake in the company of males who shared a mutual love of hunting, fishing, and telling stories. The pattern was continued in Paris as the young American with the strong midwestern work ethic and charming smile attracted a series of mentors and helpful critics who influenced and honed his writing. When he moved to Key West and then on to Cuba, the pattern of making new friends continued. However, these places also provided exciting venues for old friends to visit, and

Ernest's early letters are filled with enthusiastic invitations to "come on down" or "come on out" to hunt, fish, eat, drink, and tell stories. From his adolescence through most of his adulthood, Ernest's desire to be surrounded by his closest male friends did not vary.

Now darkness was becoming increasingly appealing. Sometime between November 1960 and January 1961 at the advice of his doctors, Ernest began electroshock treatment at the Mayo Clinic as a remedy for his depression. The treatments began with a rubber gag being placed in his mouth. Then electrodes were placed on his head and an electric current was sent to his brain. Each of the electroshock treatments produced a grand mal seizure, the equivalent of a concussion. Each time Ernest awoke, he was in a coma-like state and he was unable to say where he was or why. Given that Ernest had already suffered numerous concussions, some believe the treatment produced brain damage.[25]

After the January treatments, Ernest returned to the house in Ketchum. He tried to work on the Paris book and out of habit told Mary he was "working hard," but he couldn't write. His depression increased. When Ernest learned of the Bay of Pigs disaster and the failure of the CIA to trigger an uprising against the pro-Communist Castro regime, Ernest knew he would not be returning to Cuba.

The April 1961 Bay of Pigs Invasion had been an unsuccessful military invasion of Cuba undertaken by a counterrevolutionary military group of Cubans who were trained and funded by the U.S. government's Central Intelligence Agency (CIA). The intent of the invasion was to overthrow the revolutionary government of Fidel Castro, but the invading force was defeated within three days by the Cuban armed forces under the command of Castro. Approximately 1,334 men traveled as a seaborne force from Guatemala and an additional 177 were airborne paratroops. It's been estimated that 114 men were drowned or killed in action and another 1,183 were captured, tried, and imprisoned.

Once again, Ernest's instincts about a revolution had been correct. The failed invasion was just another example of atrocities committed on both sides of a revolution or war. He had seen it all before, especially in Spain. He now knew that he would never see his Finca, the *Pilar*, his collection of modernist paintings, his five-thousand-volume library, or his unpublished manuscripts again, and he was right. After the Bay of Pigs, the Castro government appropriated the Finca, and Ernest never returned.

Six days after the failed invasion, Mary found Ernest in the vestibule of their house, holding a shotgun and two shells. She talked with him for over an hour, until his doctor arrived and took him to the Sun Valley Hospital. After a few days in the hospital, Ernest talked his doctor into letting him go home. When he arrived at the house, he bolted out of the car, went into the house, found his shotgun, and began loading it with shells. Don Anderson, one of his hunting companions, was able to wrestle the gun away. Ernest was taken back to the Sun Valley Hospital and the next day flown to the Mayo Clinic by another friend. When the plane was being refueled in Rapid City, South Dakota, Ernest headed straight for the whirling propeller of another airplane, which stopped only after the pilot cut the engine.

Once again at the Mayo Clinic, more electric shock treatments were given. Ernest followed the doctor's orders and took daily walks, swam, and practiced target shooting. Though the shock treatments continued, Ernest eventually convinced the doctor that he was better and could go home again. He charmed the doctor and promised he would not commit suicide. When Mary arrived at the doctor's office, she was "dumbfounded to see Ernest there, dressed in his street clothes, grinning like a Cheshire cat."[26]

Mary was convinced Ernest had tricked the doctor into thinking he was OK, but didn't argue. They headed back to Ketchum by car and arrived on June 30. The next night they dined with friends at the Christiana Inn. Ernest was distracted by men he thought were FBI agents, but after a pleasant dinner they went home and slept in their separate bedrooms.

The next morning, July 2, 1961, Ernest rose before seven, left his back bedroom, and found the keys to unlock the basement door. There he picked out his double-barreled Boss shotgun from the rack and went to the upstairs foyer. Though he could no longer write, he still remembered the skill he had learned from his father, the skill he practiced in the woods of Michigan, in the green hills of Africa, and in the mountains of Idaho. He slipped two cartridges into the barrels of the gun, lowered the gun butt to the floor, pressed his forehead against the barrels, and blew away his entire cranial vault.

Ernest Hemingway in Italy practicing the skill
he learned from his father, circa 1918. *Ernest
Hemingway Foundation of Oak Park*

Chapter Seven

Places of the Soul

He looks like a modern and he smells of the museums.

—Gertrude Stein[1]

Ernest Hemingway at work on *For Whom the Bell Tolls* in Sun Valley, circa 1940. *Photofest*

ON JULY 6, 1961, FRIENDS AND FAMILY GATHERED in Ketchum, Idaho, to say good-bye to Ernest. His body was transported from the funeral home in nearby Hailey to the Ketchum Cemetery, where a small group of family members and fifty invited friends were waiting. Under blue skies with the Sawtooth Mountains as a backdrop, Father Robert J. Waldmann, the local priest, conducted a brief Catholic graveside committal service and the legendary writer was interred. Later, Bumby, John "Jack" Hemingway; Bumby's daughter, Margaux; and finally Mary would be placed in nearby graves.

Mary had asked Bill Horne to be an honorary pallbearer, and he and Bunny flew from Chicago to Salt Lake City and then went on to Ketchum. Bill brought messages of condolence from Ernest's Section IV ambulance driver friends, who had gathered for a reunion near Chicago the weekend of the suicide. Sadly, Ernest had not been invited to the reunion, and Horne was consumed with speculation of whether involvement with the reunion might have alleviated Ernest's depression and prevented his death.

However, Gianfranco Ivancich came from Venice, and Charlie Thompson traveled from Key West, and Bill Horne recalled, "Everybody who was there loved Ernie."[2] Horne also was impressed with Mary, whom he viewed as being both competent and gracious. She entertained the family at dinner the night before the service while the Hornes hosted Ernest's friends from out of town. Ernest's brother, Leicester, commented, "It seemed to me Ernest would have approved of it all."[3] As it had been with Leicester, Ernest's relationship with each of the attendees had, at some point, been confrontational. Yet almost all of them would later pen a book detailing their relationship with the man they had loved and lost.

Given Ernest's zest for living, his vast productivity as a writer, and the high profile created by his adventures and exploits, he had won and lost many friends. Long before it was over, his life's story was fertile territory for critics. Throughout his life, he longed for the approval of his parents, and they desperately tried to find some piece of his adult life or his writing of which they could approve. Yet both the son and his parents knew the closeness of the boyhood years in Oak Park would never be regained. The chasm in values and lifestyle had become too wide. Though the boyhood love of hunting and fishing provided the interest and skills for a lifetime of adventures, and the midwestern work ethic and the sound educational background in reading, writing, and the arts provided resources necessary for a successful career as a writer, once out of Oak Park, Ernest discovered cigarettes, alcohol, women, and a vocabulary that would not be tolerated in the place he once called home.

During the Paris years, the young Ernest with the engaging smile and the ability to learn quickly made friends easily. As his self-confidence grew and his fame increased, his writing and advice were increasingly in demand, but friends were won and lost along the way. Gertrude Stein had been an early mentor and friend. She encouraged Ernest to write and nurtured his appreciation of avant-garde artists and his acquisition of what turned out to be a highly valued art collection. As time passed, however, Ernest's reputation as a writer flourished and Gertrude's stalled. Still feeling the need to cast judgment, she said, "He looks like a modern and he smells of the museums."[4] The remark was meant to be critical. Yet in many ways it was a positive tribute to the depth of the content and the style of his writing.

The content of his short stories and novels is museum-like because Ernest lived in many worlds. He understood the history of his past, the literature of his past, and the pre–World War I values of his parents and grandparents. His experiences in Italy during World War I taught him that the old values no longer worked, but he was able to use the old values as a decision screen for developing the Code and creating heroes that demonstrated courage, honor, and grace under pressure in the modern world.

Because he had read all of Shakespeare and studied Dickens and Thackeray, he understood the need to develop plots that had universal meaning. Love, courage, and conflicts that showed man's struggle with nature and other men were universal themes he recreated for his novels and short stories, themes that found an audience with readers who were living in the first half of the twentieth century. These readers understood that the old rules didn't work anymore, but remembered what they were and could relate to Ernest's references to the old ideas and the quotations that still seemed to apply.

Throughout his career Ernest enhanced the content of the novels and short stories with references to classical literature. In "The

Short Happy Life of Francis Macomber," the American, Francis Macomber, discusses his fear of death with the English guide, Wilson. The guide adheres to the stoic code of a sportsman, shows courage in confronting lions, and exhibits grace under pressure. To make his point, that a man can only die but once, Ernest has Wilson quote Shakespeare, saying, "We owe God a death and let it go which way it will he that dies this year is quit for the next."[5]

After experiencing the Depression and publishing *To Have and Have Not*, the themes in Ernest's works are developed with plots where Code Heroes not only act with grace under pressure, but also believe that, as Harry Morgan would say, "no matter how a man alone ain't got no f—— chance."[6] Then, after witnessing the atrocities on both sides of the Spanish Civil War, Ernest underscores his point that men cannot act independently of one another in *For Whom the Bell Tolls*. He takes the title from a poem by John Donne, who made the same argument in the seventeenth century saying,

> No man is an island, / Entire of itself, / Every man is a piece of the continent, / A part of the main. / If a clod be washed away by the sea, / Europe is the less. / As well as if a promontory were. / As well as if a manor of thy friend's / Or of thine own were: / Any man's death diminishes me, / Because I am involved in mankind, / And therefore never send to know for whom the bell tolls; / It tolls for thee.[7]

However, Ernest did not just look to the classical English authors he found in the library of his parents' Oak Park home. He also studied and used sources from American history and ideas of American authors. The title *Across the River and into the Trees* is taken from the last words of the feisty Civil War general Stonewall Jackson, who was known to be a great strategist and military tactician. He was able to face five to one odds and still produce victory after victory. After being mortally wounded Jackson said, "Let us cross over the river and rest under the shade of the trees."[8] By referencing Jackson, Ernest was calling up the memory of the tough, brave Civil War hero who had been shot at the Battle of Chancellorsville in 1863, but survived with the loss of an arm to amputation and fought off death for eight days when he finally died of complications from pneumonia.

In using Jackson's words, Ernest tries to give depth to the character of Richard Cantwell, a battle-scarred American who was a veteran of two world wars. In this situation both the author and the main character are hoping to ride the coattails of Jackson's courageously tough reputation. As was Ernest's practice, he wrote from experience and gave Cantwell many of his own characteristics. In this case, the similarities were vast experience in war, fondness of alcohol, and being married but in love with a nineteen-year-old girl.

In addition to his knowledge of classical literature and American and European history, regular reading and study of the Bible at home and at school also enriched Ernest's writing. As young members of the Third Congregation Church, both Ernest and Marcelline were members of the Christian Endeavor Society, which offered a prize to the member who first completed reading every word of the King James Version of the Bible. Marcelline recalled that their friend, Harold Sampson, finished first in the contest, but that she and Ernest read every word of the Bible. They also "passed a detailed test on the Bible and . . . both learned a lot."[9]

Similarly, study of the Bible also was required at Oak Park High School. For many years the curriculum of freshman English classes included Bible stories, the rationale being that students would better understand biblical allusions in American and English literature studied junior and senior years.

Given Ernest's background it's not surprising that biblical references are embedded in his writing. He had a thorough understanding of the Bible, understood how biblical references could enrich literature, and believed that reading the Bible taught a storyteller the art of the narrative.

The title *The Sun Also Rises* comes from Ecclesiastes 1:4–5: "One generation passeth away, and another generation cometh: but the earth abideth for ever. The sun also ariseth, and the sun goeth down, and hasteth to his place where he arose."[10]

Though the novel focuses on the dissipation of the expatriate crowd Ernest encountered in the Montparnasse area of Paris, the plot and characters in the novel offer a two-pronged solution to facing one's ultimate end, death. Some of the characters are lost. They are the "rotten crowd" of Montparnasse. They had observed

the horrors of trench warfare and the use of chemical weapons
and found it difficult to believe that God could allow such horror
and waste of human life. For the characters who represented the
lost generation, traditional Christian morality no longer had any
relevance. They knew the world had changed and the old rules no
longer worked. They were unsure what the changes meant, so they
drank to excess and were promiscuous.

However, the novel also can be viewed from the perspective of
a protagonist who searches for integrity in a decadent and depraved
world. In a sense, Jake is the moral center of the story. He is not
part of the expatriate crowd, but a working man who is trying to
bear himself well in the postwar ruins. His model for a life of action, ritual, and courage is the bullfighter, Pedro Romero. He is the
hero in the ring, who bravely faces death. Though the novel is about
a generation that is lost, it offers hope through the characters of
Jake Barnes and Pedro Romero. It is through them the reader learns
that "the sun also ariseth" and that "the earth abideth for ever."

Ernest also used his knowledge of the Bible and his Christian
background to develop the theme and main character in *The Old
Man and the Sea*, and much has been written about his use of
Christian symbolism in the novel. Though Ernest did not believe in
overt use of symbols and disliked talking about them, he did believe
that symbols were a "measure of what [the reader] brought to the
reading."[11] Given his own Christian background, he makes it easy
for a Christian reader to compare the incidents that take place during the progression of the plot to those in the life of Jesus. Both the
old man, Santiago, and Jesus were fishermen; both suffer in many
of the same ways; and both ultimately face death with a quiet sto-
icism. After Santiago catches the marlin, he faces the attack of the
sharks and the possibility of death with grace under pressure. Like
Jesus, his suffering is quiet. When he first sees the sharks, he says
only, "'Ay.' . . . There is no translation for this word and perhaps it
is just a noise such as a man might make, involuntarily, feeling the
nail go through his hands and into the wood."[12]

As plot of the novel progresses, there also are additional parallels to the crucifixion of Jesus. Santiago's hands with "the deep-
creased scars from handling heavy fish on the cords"[13] and "with a

line burn that had cut his flesh"[14] evoke the hands of the crucified Jesus. Then, once back on shore, Santiago climbs the hill to his shack with the mast on his shoulder, falls, and "lays for some time with the mast across his shoulder."[15] Finally, when Santiago makes his way into his shack, he collapses into his bed with "his arms out straight and the palms of his hands up."[16] He is positioned as Jesus was on the cross.

In his novels and short stories, Ernest writes of the horrors of modern life: death, war, the Depression, and loss, whether it be the loss of a loved one, such as Catherine in *A Farewell to Arms*, or the loss of a valued trophy, such as the marlin in *The Old Man and the Sea*. In each work, it is the Code that charts the possibility of a way out with dignity, how an individual may be "destroyed but not defeated."[17] In each work, the means for confronting the horrors of life are infused with the words and the wisdom of the past.

How man confronts death is the ultimate focus of Ernest's novels and short stories. He contemplates how people behave in the presence of death and basically offers two solutions. In his first novel, *The Sun Also Rises*, he portrays the "lost generation" who escape death by not really thinking about it. Their world is one of dissipation and senselessness. They numb their senses with alcohol and promiscuity. The alternative path described in the novel is the better, more stoic solution. It is the world of the good matador who exhibits grace under pressure and is a model for confronting death with honor and courage.

A Farewell to Arms, though in a different setting, follows a similar theme. Ernest details the horror, confusion, and irrationality of modern warfare as the carabinieri randomly pull officers from the columns of retreating men and execute them on sight. The first "solution" is in the form of the zealous patriotism of the carabinieri. Their senselessness and cruelty in the name of patriotism is irrational. Similarly, the officer who is resigned to his defeat and neither flees nor protests his execution also seems foolishly patriotic.

The alternative is presented by Code Hero Frederic Henry, who confronts death with courage and makes his separate "common sense" peace by escaping from the senseless acts of the carabinieri. Knowing he will be next, Frederic flees not out of cowardice, but from his refusal to die for a cause that, to him, seems meaningless. He strips himself of the stars that mark him as a lieutenant and jumps into the river. Ernest's use of the natural symbol of the river becomes a Christian baptism of sorts. By jumping into the river, Frederic's "anger was washed away . . . along with any obligation."[18] After he meets Catherine in Stresa, they row across the lake to Switzerland. Frederic's hands become blistered and raw, but he admits, "There's no hole in my side."[19]

The smell of the museum not only contributed to the content and metaphors of Ernest's novels and short stories, it also influenced his economic style of writing. Because he knew the old rules, he was able to break them. He understood the boredom that came from endless description and he didn't tell his readers what to think. His Code Heroes spoke and acted according to the new rules. It was up to the reader to understand without endless explanation. Reading the work of Mark Twain, Ernest had learned the value of dialogue and honest language. In *Green Hills of Africa*, he concluded that all American literature began with *Huckleberry Finn*.

However, breaking the old rules didn't mean one could be careless—maybe in letters to friends and family, but not in serious writing. While his powers of observation were honed by his experiences in journalism, his understanding of grammar and usage was honed by the standards set by the *Kansas City Star*. Young reporters were required to follow the *Star Copy Style Sheet*, which asked reporters to use short sentences, short first paragraphs, and vigorous English and eliminate every superfluous word.[20] Ernest later said that the 110 rules were the "best rules [he] ever learned for the business of writing. [He had] never forgotten them."[21]

Eventually, Ernest settled on what he called "the principle of the iceberg."[22] When talking about the way in which he wrote, he said,

> There is seven-eighths of it under water for every part that shows. Anything you know you can eliminate and it only strengthens your iceberg. . . . So I have tried to eliminate everything unnecessary to conveying experience to the reader so that after he or she has read something it will become a part of his or her experience

and seem actually to have happened. This is very hard to do and I've worked at it very hard.[23]

Because his parents and Gertrude Stein were significant influences in Ernest's early life and his development as a writer, he probably took their criticisms or lack of acceptance of his writing more seriously than the criticism of others. His letters to his parents indicate that he was hurt by their responses to his early publication, *in our time*, and that he eventually tried to explain to them that he was writing about "the bad and the ugly as well as what is beautiful."[24] His letter, however, did not negate the hurt that came from his father's return of all six copies of *in our time* to the Three Mountains Press in Paris or from his father saying he was

> incensed that a son of his would so far forget his Christian training that he could use the subject matter and vulgar expressions this book contained, . . . [that] no gentleman spoke of venereal disease outside a doctor's office. . . . He would not tolerate such filth in his home.[25]

Ernest's comments to Ezra Pound also indicate that he was hurt by Gertrude Stein's criticism and felt the need to reply. After she said, "He looks like a modern and he smells of the museums,"[26] he wrote to Ezra Pound, saying, "I stuck by the old bitch until she threw me out of the house when she lost her judgment with the menopause, but it seems that I'm just a fickle, brittle brain-picking bastard. She gave me some damned good advice many times and much shit to boot."[27]

However, Ernest's parents and Stein were not his only critics. *In Our Time, Men without Women*, and *The Sun Also Rises* were viewed by some as the "sordid little catastrophes in the lives of very vulgar people."[28] The criticism of these early works was based on Ernest's honest portrayal of life in the 1920s and the critics' misunderstanding of his basic values. While he tried to honestly portray the prostitutes, the drug fiends, and the rotten crowd of Montparnasse, there was an underlying disdain of the rotten crowd that really was symptomatic of his midwestern American values. Ernest worked hard himself and admired the hard work of others. He portrayed Jake Barnes and the matadors and the prostitutes, who worked for a living, in a positive manner, but was more disapproving of Brett and the others in her group, who lived on inherited money.

After Ernest returned to Oak Park from Italy, he seemed to have a need to show his readers what he had told his sister: "There's a whole big world out there full of people who really feel things."[29] Once he left Oak Park, he discovered a new world that was inhabited by people he never would have met in Oak Park. Exploring that world beyond Oak Park remained important throughout his career. He traveled down a miraculous path of discovery: Paris, Switzerland, Pamplona, East Africa, the Gulf Stream, China, and Cuba. To some extent, it seems as though he just wanted to share his discoveries with the folks back home, regardless of how shocking they might be to them.

In his early short stories and novels as well as his articles for the *Toronto Star*, Ernest tended to divide his characters into people of action, such as his Code Heroes, and people of inaction, such as those who sat around and intellectualized or failed to take action out of fear. In the first category, he included bullfighters, soldiers, and common working people; in the second category he placed cowards, effete writers and artists, politicians, and wealthy, spoiled women. Compared to Oak Park, it was a sordid little world. But the reaction to his characters and their lives was eventually positive. His critics would soon write that "Hemingway's people were immoral, drank too much, had no religion or ideals," but "have courage and friendship, and mental honestness. And they are *alive*. Amazingly real and alive."[30]

During the Depression, Ernest had to weather a different sort of criticism. Though he had accumulated significant fame and an admirable reputation as an American writer, he had been secluded in Key West and his critics became critical of his subject matter, especially in *Death in the Afternoon* and *Green Hills of Africa*. *Death in the Afternoon* was criticized as an elitist, aristocratic bullfighting book, and Granville Hicks found the big game hunting in *Green Hills of Africa* "trivial and dull."[31] The United States was in a depression, and the subject matter of both books was criticized because more important things were happening in the world. With millions of people out of work, bullfighting, big game hunting, and marlin fishing were viewed as escapist and elitist.

Ernest never really engaged in politics. He believed "there [is] not left and right in writing. There is only good and bad writing."[32] He thought that involvement with politics could distract a writer from his main purpose of seeing and presenting the world clearly because a writer who gave priority to political causes could not be objective. However, he did take a more leftist stance after the hurricane of 1935 hit the Florida Keys by writing *To Have and Have Not*.

Though Ernest's work during and after the Depression shows his belief that "no matter how a man alone ain't got no f—— chance";[33] that "no man is an island, entire of itself";[34] he embraced neither the ideals nor the reforms of the New Deal. He was suspicious of reformers and governmental bureaucracies because they tried to control human beings, often demeaning their self-respect, dignity, and sense of honor. As FERA moved into Key West to provide relief to the victims of the Depression, Ernest viewed the federal bureaucrats as "starry eyed bastards spending money that somebody will have to pay."[35] He noted the transformation in his beloved Key West, saying, "Everybody in our town quit work to go on relief. Fishermen all turned carpenters. Reverse of the Bible."[36]

Though Ernest wrote a "leftist" book, he continued to support many of his family's values, especially those that embraced self-reliance and were skeptical of governmental relief for private citizens. His views resembled those of Grandfather Anson, who said he would never knowingly sit at a table with a Democrat.

While the United States worked its way out of the Depression, Ernest directed his interests and efforts to reporting on the Spanish Civil War and eventually World War II. Though he wasn't allowed to carry a weapon, he threw himself into frontline situations and reported the military action with the detail and honesty that had become characteristic of his writing. His work as a war correspondent was highly respected and widely published. In 1947 he received a Bronze Star and was recognized for his bravery "under fire in combat areas in order to obtain an accurate picture of conditions."[37]

When he returned to Cuba after World War II, he not only was an acclaimed writer, he also was a legendary citizen of the world with many responsibilities and demands. There were the demands of ex-wives and children as well as the responsibilities of managing financial assets, royalties from around the world, real estate, and numerous requests for movie rights and articles. With his successes there also were lapses in what had become his characteristic good judgment about subject matter and discipline in style.

Across the River and into the Trees did not meet the expectations of those who believed Ernest was "the most important author living today."[38] The story of an aging war hero in love with a teenager didn't sit well with most critics. Though some said Ernest's "grasp of contemporary situations [was] . . . profound and decade ahead of his public's,"[39] others felt "embarrassment and even pity, that so important a writer [could] make such a travesty of himself."[40] Ernest had played the role of a foolish middle-aged man when he became so infatuated with Adriana and then committed his foolishness to paper. It was the lapse in judgment of a now legendary writer and viewed by almost everyone but Ernest as a disaster. Despite the negative reviews, however, the book sold out the initial printing of seventy-five thousand copies and was on the *New York Times* best-seller list for twenty-one weeks.

Fortunately, the reviews set him straight. He was hurt by the critics and felt the need to rescue his reputation. He regained his focus and wrote *The Old Man and the Sea*. Writing in the mornings, he penned a story about an old man who is down on his luck and wrestles victory out of defeat. Readers and critics quickly saw the parallels to Ernest's life. Like the old man, Ernest, too, was a former champion trying to make a comeback. Some thought the attack of the sharks symbolized the attack of the critics on *Across the River and into the Trees*. However, Ernest, trying to distance himself from the critics and their interpretations, said no, that he was simply writing about sharks.

Whether the parallels between Ernest and the old man were deliberate or not, the book was a success. *Life* published the book in its entirety and never before had an author reached so large an audience. Then Scribner's published a first edition of fifty thousand copies, which sold out in ten days, and the Book of the Month Club published 153,000 copies. Within five years the book was translated into twenty-six languages, including Persian. Both Ernest and the old man had proved that "man is not made for defeat."[41]

After the trip to Spain and Africa, Ernest and Mary returned to the Finca, and it was there on October 28, 1954, that Ernest learned he had been awarded the Nobel Prize. Because of his declining health and his dislike of formal speeches, he did not attend the ceremony in Stockholm. Rather he sent a written statement to be read by John Cabot, the American ambassador to Sweden. In his comments, he mentioned two lifelong habits. First, he told his audience that

> writing, at its best, is a lonely life. Organizations for writers palliate the writer's loneliness but I doubt if they improve his writing. He grows in public stature as he sheds his loneliness and often his work deteriorates. For he does his work alone and if he is a good enough writer he must face eternity, or the lack of it, each day.[42]

The first habit, the ability to tolerate the lonely life of writing, reflects the disciplined work ethic Ernest learned as a child. The Oak Park homes were places where the focus was on work and service to mankind. Ernest's father did not tolerate just sitting around. His children had to be reading a book, studying, or doing something worthwhile. It's not surprising that Ernest developed a code of behavior for life in the modern world because he had grown up with a strict code of behavior. His father had set rules, and the children were spanked if they infringed on one that was considered essential.

Though Ernest certainly learned how to play in his adult life, he was happiest when he was writing. He always followed a strict pattern of behavior for his written work, and in 1954 described his writing routine to George Plimpton, saying,

> When I am working on a book or a story I write every morning as soon after first light as possible. There is no one to disturb you and it is cool or cold and you come to your work and warm as you write. You read what you have written and, as you always stop when you know what is going to happen next; you go on from there. You write until you come to a place where you still have your juice and know what will happen next.[43]

The second lifelong habit that emerged in his Nobel Prize acceptance speech was his lifelong interest in reading and his background in classical literature. He tells his audience,

> For a true writer each book should be a new beginning where he tries again for something that is beyond attainment. He should always try for something that has never been done or that others have tried and failed. Then sometimes, with great luck, he will succeed.
>
> How simple the writing of literature would be if it were only necessary to write in another way what has been well written. It is because we have had such great writers in the past that a writer is driven far out past where he can go, out to where no one can help him.[44]

Ernest had a thorough knowledge of "great writers in the past." Reading books at home, at the library, at school, and at Walloon Lake was an important part of his childhood. A visit to any of his houses also reinforces how reading contributed to Ernest's adult life and continuing education. There are books everywhere—living rooms, bedrooms, bathrooms, as well as formal library settings. Similarly, reading any of his novels or short stories reveals how his knowledge of literature brought depth to the themes of his work and the dialogue of his characters.

Ernest's work ethic and his love of reading were habits learned in Oak Park. Though many of his values changed, those two habits remained. Much of his success was based on his midwestern work ethic and his refusal to give up, regardless of the hurt. His early education and his persistence in reading the best literature also gave him the knowledge and the motivation to "write in another way." Though by the end of his life, Ernest's separation from Oak Park was quite complete, the love, the discipline, and the education he received there provided him with a sense of self-confidence, discipline, and spirit of adventure that lasted his entire life.

Notes

Chapter One

1. Maria Montessori, quoted in "Maria Montessori Quotes," *Daily Montessori*, 2011, www.dailymontessori.com/maria-montessor-quotes .html (accessed June 21, 2012).

2. Ernest Hemingway, Letter to Fritz Saviers, June 15, 1961, in *Ernest Hemingway: Selected Letters, 1917–1961*, ed. C. Baker (New York: Scribner's, 1981), 921. Reprinted with the permission of Scribner Publishing Group from ERNEST HEMINGWAY, SELECTED LETTERS 1917–1961 edited by Carlos Baker. Copyright © 1981 by Carlos Baker and The Ernest Hemingway Foundation, Inc. All rights reserved.

3. Ernest Hemingway, "Indian Camp," *The Nick Adams Stories* (New York: Charles Scribner's Sons, 1972), 21. Reprinted with the permission of Scribner Publishing Group from THE NICK ADAMS STORIES by Ernest Hemingway. Copyright © 1972 and renewed © 2000 by The Ernest Hemingway Foundation. All rights reserved.

4. Hemingway, "Indian Camp," *The Nick Adams Stories*, 21. Reprinted with the permission of Scribner Publishing Group from THE NICK AD-AMS STORIES by Ernest Hemingway. Copyright © 1972 and renewed © 2000 by The Ernest Hemingway Foundation. All rights reserved.

5. Ernest Hemingway, *A Moveable Feast* (New York: Charles Scribner's Sons, 1964), 44–45. Reprinted with the permission of Scribner Publishing Group from A MOVEABLE FEAST by Ernest Hemingway. Copyright © 1964 by Ernest Hemingway. Copyright renewed © 1992 by John H.

Hemingway, Patrick Hemingway, and Gregory Hemingway. All rights reserved.

6. Ernest Hemingway, "Fathers and Sons," *The Nick Adams Stories* (New York: Charles Scribner's Sons, 1972), 258. Reprinted with the permission of Scribner Publishing Group from THE NICK ADAMS STORIES by Ernest Hemingway. Copyright © 1972 and renewed © 2000 by The Ernest Hemingway Foundation. All rights reserved.

7. Ernest Hemingway, "Fathers and Sons," *The Nick Adams Stories*, 264–65. Reprinted with the permission of Scribner Publishing Group from THE NICK ADAMS STORIES by Ernest Hemingway. Copyright © 1972 and renewed © 2000 by The Ernest Hemingway Foundation. All rights reserved.

8. Ernest Hemingway, quoted in "Hemingway Here, Avid for Lion Hunt," *New York Times*, April 4, 1934, www.nytimes.com/books.99/07/04/specials/hemingway-lionhunt.html (accessed June 22, 2012).

9. Philip Young, *Ernest Hemingway: A Reconsideration* (New York: Harcourt, Brace & World, 1966), 63.

10. Ernest Hemingway, "Indian Camp," *The Nick Adams Stories*, 19. Reprinted with the permission of Scribner Publishing Group from THE NICK ADAMS STORIES by Ernest Hemingway. Copyright © 1972 and renewed © 2000 by The Ernest Hemingway Foundation. All rights reserved.

11. Ernest Hemingway, *A Farewell to Arms* (New York: Charles Scribner's Sons, 1929), 55–56. Reprinted with the permission of Scribner Publishing Group from A FAREWELL TO ARMS by Ernest Hemingway. Copyright © 1929 by Charles Scribner's Sons. Copyright renewed © 1957 by Ernest Hemingway. All rights reserved.

12. Anson Hemingway, *Civil War Journal*, May 1863, Special Collections, Oak Park Public Library, Oak Park, Illinois.

13. Paul Hendrickson, *Hemingway's Boat* (New York: Knopf, 2011), 144.

14. Fannie Biggs, *Memories of Ernest Hemingway*, Charles Fenton papers, February 24, 1952, Yale Collection of American Literature, Beinecke Rare Book and Manuscript Library, Yale University.

15. Clarence Hemingway, Letter to Ernest Hemingway, July 29, 1915, Hemingway Collection, John F. Kennedy Library, Boston.

16. Grace Hall Hemingway, *Memory Book I*, Hemingway Collection, John F. Kennedy Library, Boston.

17. Grace Hall Hemingway, *Memory Book I*.

18. Grace Hall Hemingway, *Memory Book I*.

19. Ernest (Abba) Hall, quoted in Marcelline Sanford, *At the Hemingways* (Moscow: University of Idaho Press, 1999), 12.

20. Ernest Hemingway, "Now I Lay Me," *The Nick Adams Stories*, 146–47. Reprinted with the permission of Scribner Publishing Group from THE NICK ADAMS STORIES by Ernest Hemingway. Copyright © 1972 and renewed © 2000 by The Ernest Hemingway Foundation. All rights reserved.

21. Ernest Hemingway, "Hi Lights and Lo Lights," *Trapeze*, 1916.

22. Ernest Hemingway, "A Ring Lardner on the Bloomington Game," *Trapeze*, 1916.

23. Fannie Biggs, quoted in Peter Griffin, *Along with Youth* (New York: Oxford University Press, 1985), 25.

24. Ernest Hemingway, *Green Hills of Africa* (New York: Charles Scribner's Sons, 1935), 22. Reprinted with the permission of Scribner Publishing Group from GREEN HILLS OF AFRICA by Ernest Hemingway. Copyright © 1935 by Charles Scribner's Sons. Copyright renewed © 1963 by Mary Hemingway. All rights reserved.

25. Ernest Hemingway, quoted in Griffin, *Along with Youth*, 41.

26. Ernest Hemingway, quoted in Sheridan Baker, *Ernest Hemingway: An Introduction and Interpretation* (Ann Arbor: University of Michigan, 1967), 10.

27. Pete Wellington, quoted in Carlos Baker, *Ernest Hemingway: A Life Story* (New York: Charles Scribner's Sons, 1969), 34.

28. Ernest Hemingway, quoted in Sanford, *At the Hemingways*, 156–57.

29. Clarence Hemingway, Letter to Ernest Hemingway, April 17, 1918, Hemingway Collection, John F. Kennedy Library, Boston.

30. Grace Hall Hemingway, Letter to Ernest Hemingway, April 17, 1918, Hemingway Collection, John F. Kennedy Library, Boston.

31. Ernest Hemingway, quoted in Fannie Biggs, *Memories of Ernest Hemingway*, Charles Fenton Papers (no date), Yale Collection of American Literature, Beinecke Rare Book and Manuscript Library, Yale University.

32. Milford Baker, *Milford Baker Diary*, June 7, 1918, Carlos Baker papers.

33. Ernest Hemingway, *Death in the Afternoon* (New York: Charles Scribner's Sons, 1932), 135–36. Reprinted with the permission of Scribner Publishing Group from DEATH IN THE AFTERNOON by Ernest Hemingway. Copyright © 1932 by Charles Scribner's Sons. Copyright renewed © 1960 by Ernest Hemingway. All rights reserved.

34. Bill Horne, quoted in Virginia Moseley, "Hemingway Remembered," *Barrington Courier Review*, September 27, 1979, 28–33.

35. Robert Lewis, "Hemingway in Italy," *Journal of Modern Literature* (May 1982): 215.

36. Clarence Hemingway, Letter to Ernest Hemingway, July 17, 1918, Hemingway Collection, John F. Kennedy Library, Boston.

37. Ernest Hemingway, *A Farewell to Arms*, 55–56. Reprinted with the permission of Scribner Publishing Group from A FAREWELL TO ARMS by Ernest Hemingway. Copyright © 1929 by Charles Scribner's Sons. Copyright renewed © 1957 by Ernest Hemingway. All rights reserved.

38. Ernest Hemingway, Letter to Grace Hall Hemingway, July 19, 1918, quoted in H. Villard and J. Nagel, *Hemingway in Love and War: The Lost Diary of Agnes Von Kurowsky* (Boston: Northeastern University Press, 1989), 170.

39. Ernest Hemingway, *A Farewell to Arms*, 72. Reprinted with the permission of Scribner Publishing Group from A FAREWELL TO ARMS by Ernest Hemingway. Copyright © 1929 by Charles Scribner's Sons. Copyright renewed © 1957 by Ernest Hemingway. All rights reserved.

40. Ernest Hemingway quoted in James Mellow, *Hemingway: A Life without Consequences* (New York: Addison-Wesley, 1992), 65.

41. Agnes von Kurowsky, *Agnes von Kurowsky Diary*, quoted in Villard and Nagel, *Hemingway in Love and War*, 62.

42. Agnes von Kurowsky, *Agnes von Kurowsky Diary*, quoted in Villard and Nagel, *Hemingway in Love and War*, 77.

43. Ernest Hemingway, *A Farewell to Arms*, 114. Reprinted with the permission of Scribner Publishing Group from A FAREWELL TO ARMS by Ernest Hemingway. Copyright © 1929 by Charles Scribner's Sons. Copyright renewed © 1957 by Ernest Hemingway. All rights reserved.

44. Ernest Hemingway, Letter to Bill Horne, March 13, 1919, Ernest Hemingway Foundation of Oak Park Collection.

45. Bill Horne, quoted in Moseley, "Hemingway Remembered."

46. Frank Platt, "Hemingway's Oak Park Years," Panel Discussion at Triton College, River Grove, Illinois, September 24, 1974.

47. Sanford, *At the Hemingways*, 184.

48. Ernest Hemingway, Letter to Jim Gamble, March 3, 1919, in *Ernest Hemingway: Selected Letters 1917–1961*, ed. C. Baker, 22. Reprinted with the permission of Scribner Publishing Group from ERNEST HEMINGWAY, SELECTED LETTERS 1917–1961 edited by Carlos Baker. Copyright © 1981 by Carlos Baker and The Ernest Hemingway Foundation, Inc. All rights reserved.

49. Agnes von Kurowsky, Letter to Ernest Hemingway, March 7, 1919, Ernest Hemingway Foundation Collection, Oak Park, Illinois.

50. M. Dietrich, "The Most Fascinating Man I Know," *New York Herald Tribune*, February 13, 1955, 8–9. TM & © Marlene, Inc. All Rights Reserved.

Chapter Two

1. Marcelline Hemingway Sanford, *At the Hemingways* (Moscow: University of Idaho Press, 1999), 184.

2. Ernest Hemingway, *A Farewell to Arms* (New York: Charles Scribner's Sons, 1929), 20. Reprinted with the permission of Scribner Publishing Group from A FAREWELL TO ARMS by Ernest Hemingway. Copyright © 1929 by Charles Scribner's Sons. Copyright renewed © 1957 by Ernest Hemingway. All rights reserved.

3. Sanford, *At the Hemingways*, 105.

4. Ernest Hemingway, Letter to Family, January 15, 1920, Lilly Library, Indiana University, quoted in M. Reynolds, *The Paris Years* (Cambridge, MA: Basil Blackwell, 1980), 17.

5. Ernest Hemingway, *A Movable Feast* (New York: Charles Scribner's Sons, 1964), 12. Reprinted with the permission of Scribner Publishing Group from A MOVEABLE FEAST by Ernest Hemingway. Copyright © 1964 by Ernest Hemingway. Copyright renewed © 1992 by John H. Hemingway, Patrick Hemingway, and Gregory Hemingway. All rights reserved.

6. Ernest Hemingway, "Clemenceau Politically Dead," in *Dateline: Toronto*, ed. W. White (New York: Charles Scribner's Sons, 1985), 94. Reprinted with the permission of Scribner Publishing Group from ERNEST HEMINGWAY: DATELINE: TORONTO edited by William White. Copyright © 1985 by Mary Hemingway, John Hemingway, Patrick Hemingway, and Gregory Hemingway. All rights reserved.

7. Hemingway, "Clemenccau Politically Dead," in *Dateline: Toronto*, 94. Reprinted with the permission of Scribner Publishing Group from ERNEST HEMINGWAY: DATELINE: TORONTO edited by William White. Copyright © 1985 by Mary Hemingway, John Hemingway, Patrick Hemingway, and Gregory Hemingway. All rights reserved.

8. Ernest Hemingway, "Try Bobsledding if You Want Thrills," in *Dateline: Toronto*, 101–2. Reprinted with the permission of Scribner Publishing Group from ERNEST HEMINGWAY: DATELINE: TORONTO edited by William White. Copyright © 1985 by Mary Hemingway, John Hemingway, Patrick Hemingway, and Gregory Hemingway. All rights reserved.

9. Ernest Hemingway, Letter to Max Perkins, March 17, 1928, in *Ernest Hemingway: Selected Letters, 1917–1961*, ed. Carlos Baker (New York: Scribner's, 1981), 273. Reprinted with the permission of Scribner Publishing Group from ERNEST HEMINGWAY, SELECTED LETTERS 1917–1961 edited by Carlos Baker. Copyright © 1981 by Carlos Baker and The Ernest Hemingway Foundation, Inc. All rights reserved.

10. Hemingway, *A Farewell to Arms*, 291. Reprinted with the permission of Scribner Publishing Group from A FAREWELL TO ARMS by Ernest Hemingway. Copyright © 1929 by Charles Scribner's Sons. Copyright renewed © 1957 by Ernest Hemingway. All rights reserved.

11. Ernest Hemingway, "A Silent, Ghastly Procession," in *Dateline: Toronto*, 232. Reprinted with the permission of Scribner Publishing Group from ERNEST HEMINGWAY: DATELINE: TORONTO edited by William White. Copyright © 1985 by Mary Hemingway, John Hemingway, Patrick Hemingway, and Gregory Hemingway. All rights reserved.

12. Ernest Hemingway, "Mussolini, Europe's Prize Bluffer," in *Dateline: Toronto*, 253–59. Reprinted with the permission of Scribner Publishing Group from ERNEST HEMINGWAY: DATELINE: TORONTO edited by William White. Copyright © 1985 by Mary Hemingway, John Hemingway, Patrick Hemingway, and Gregory Hemingway. All rights reserved.

13. Hemingway, "Mussolini, Europe's Prize Bluffer," in *Dateline: Toronto*, 253–59. Reprinted with the permission of Scribner Publishing Group from ERNEST HEMINGWAY: DATELINE: TORONTO edited by William White. Copyright © 1985 by Mary Hemingway, John Hemingway, Patrick Hemingway, and Gregory Hemingway. All rights reserved.

14. Hemingway, "Mussolini, Europe's Prize Bluffer," 253–59. Reprinted with the permission of Scribner Publishing Group from ERNEST HEMINGWAY: DATELINE: TORONTO edited by William White. Copyright © 1985 by Mary Hemingway, John Hemingway, Patrick Hemingway, and Gregory Hemingway. All rights reserved.

15. Ernest Hemingway, "American Bohemians in Paris," in *Dateline: Toronto*, 114–15. Reprinted with the permission of Scribner Publishing Group from ERNEST HEMINGWAY: DATELINE: TORONTO edited by William White. Copyright © 1985 by Mary Hemingway, John Hemingway, Patrick Hemingway, and Gregory Hemingway. All rights reserved.

16. Sanford, *At the Hemingways*, 322.

17. Sanford, *At the Hemingways*, 322.

18. Grace Hall Hemingway, quoted in Reynolds, *The Paris Years*, 191.

19. Ernest Hemingway, Letter to Clarence Hemingway, March 20, 1925, in *Ernest Hemingway: Selected Letters*, 153. Reprinted with the permission of Scribner Publishing Group from ERNEST HEMINGWAY, SELECTED LETTERS 1917–1961 edited by Carlos Baker. Copyright © 1981 by Carlos Baker and The Ernest Hemingway Foundation, Inc. All rights reserved.

20. Ernest Hemingway, "The Three-Day Blow," in *In Our Time* (Charles Scribner's Sons, 1925), 46. Reprinted with the permission of Scribner Pub-

21. Ernest Hemingway, "Up in Michigan," in *Three Stories and Ten
Poems*, (Paris: Contact Publishing, 1923).

22. Ernest Hemingway, Letter to Family, May 1924, Lilly Library, Indiana University, quoted in Reynolds, *The Paris Years*, 177.

23. *The Holy Bible*, Ecclesiastes 1:4–5.

24. Ernest Hemingway, *The Sun Also Rises* (New York: Charles
Scribner's Sons, 1926), 115.

25. Grace Hall Hemingway to Ernest Hemingway, quoted in Kenneth
Lynn, *Hemingway* (New York: Simon and Schuster, 1987), 357.

26. Clarence Hemingway to Ernest Hemingway, December, 19, 1926,
quoted in J. Mellow, *Hemingway: A Life without Consequences* (New York:
Addison-Wesley, 1992), 336.

CHAPTER THREE

1. Grace Hall Hemingway, *Memory Book I*, Hemingway Collection,
John F. Kennedy Library, Boston.

2. Grace Hall Hemingway, *Memory Book I*.

3. Grace Hall Hemingway, *Memory Book I*.

4. Marcelline Hemingway Sanford, *At the Hemingways* (Moscow: University of Idaho Press), 79.

5. Sanford, *At the Hemingways*, 75.

6. H. Donnelly and R. Billings, *Sara & Gerald* (New York: Times Books,
1982), 22.

7. Ernest Hemingway, Letter to F. Scott Fitzgerald, October 30, 1927,
quoted in J. Mellow, *Hemingway: A Life without Consequences* (New York:
Addison-Wesley, 1992), 358.

8. Ernest Hemingway, Letter to Ezra Pound, July 19, 1924, in *Ernest
Hemingway: Selected Letters, 1917–1961*, ed. Carlos Baker (New York:
Scribner's, 1981), 119.

9. Ernest Hemingway, Letter to Ernest Walsh, January 1926, quoted in Mellow, *Hemingway: A Life without Consequences*, 323.

10. Matthew Nickel, "Young Hemingway's Wound and Conversion," *Pilgrim*, March 2013, 6.

11. Ernest Hemingway, *A Moveable Feast* (New York: Charles Scribner's Sons, 1964), 210. Reprinted with the permission of Scribner Publishing Group from A MOVEABLE FEAST by Ernest Hemingway. Copyright © 1964 by Ernest Hemingway. Copyright renewed © 1992 by John H. Hemingway, Patrick Hemingway, and Gregory Hemingway. All rights reserved.

12. Mellow, *Hemingway: A Life without Consequences*, 358.

13. Conard Aiken, *New York Times*, quoted in Mellow, *Hemingway: A Life without Consequences*, 334.

14. Ernest Hemingway to A. E. Hotchner, in A. E. Hotchner, *Hemingway and His World* (New York: Vendome Press, 1989), 108.

15. Clarence Hemingway, Letter to Ernest Hemingway, June 4, 1928, Hemingway Collection, John F. Kennedy Library.

16. Ernest Hemingway, Letter to Max Perkins, July 23, 1928, in *Ernest Hemingway: Selected Letters, 1917–1961*, 280. Reprinted with the permission of Scribner Publishing Group from ERNEST HEMINGWAY, SELECTED LETTERS 1917–1961 edited by Carlos Baker. Copyright © 1981 by Carlos Baker and The Ernest Hemingway Foundation, Inc. All rights reserved.

17. Ernest Hemingway, Letter to Guy Hickok, July 27, 1928, in *Ernest Hemingway: Selected Letters, 1917–1961*, 280. Reprinted with the permission of Scribner Publishing Group from ERNEST HEMINGWAY, SELECTED LETTERS 1917–1961 edited by Carlos Baker. Copyright © 1981 by Carlos Baker and The Ernest Hemingway Foundation, Inc. All rights reserved.

18. Leicester Hemingway, *My Brother, Ernest Hemingway* (Cleveland: World, 1962), 111.

19. Ernest Hemingway, Letter to F. Scott Fitzgerald, December 9, 1928, in *Ernest Hemingway: Selected Letters, 1917–1961*, 291. Reprinted with the permission of Scribner Publishing Group from ERNEST HEMINGWAY, SELECTED LETTERS 1917–1961 edited by Carlos Baker. Copyright © 1981 by Carlos Baker and The Ernest Hemingway Foundation, Inc. All rights reserved.

20. Ernest Hemingway, Letter to Max Perkins, December 16, 1928, in *Ernest Hemingway: Selected Letters, 1917–1961*, 291. Reprinted with the permission of Scribner Publishing Group from ERNEST HEMINGWAY, SELECTED LETTERS 1917–1961 edited by Carlos Baker. Copyright ©

1981 by Carlos Baker and The Ernest Hemingway Foundation, Inc. All rights reserved.

21. Ernest Hemingway, Letter to Grace Hall Hemingway, March 11, 1929, in *Ernest Hemingway: Selected Letters, 1917–1961*, 295. Reprinted with the permission of Scribner Publishing Group from ERNEST HEMINGWAY, SELECTED LETTERS 1917–1961 edited by Carlos Baker. Copyright © 1981 by Carlos Baker and The Ernest Hemingway Foundation, Inc. All rights reserved.

22. Leicester Hemingway, *My Brother, Ernest Hemingway*, 109–10.

23. Ernest Hemingway, Letter to Max Perkins, January 8, 1929, in *Ernest Hemingway: Selected Letters, 1917–1961*, 292. Reprinted with the permission of Scribner Publishing Group from ERNEST HEMINGWAY, SELECTED LETTERS 1917–1961 edited by Carlos Baker. Copyright © 1981 by Carlos Baker and The Ernest Hemingway Foundation, Inc. All rights reserved.

24. Ernest Hemingway, Letter to John Dos Passos, February 9, 1929, in *Ernest Hemingway: Selected Letters, 1917–1961*, 295. Reprinted with the permission of Scribner Publishing Group from ERNEST HEMINGWAY, SELECTED LETTERS 1917–1961 edited by Carlos Baker. Copyright © 1981 by Carlos Baker and The Ernest Hemingway Foundation, Inc. All rights reserved.

25. Grace Hall Hemingway, Letter to Ernest Hemingway, quoted in Mellow, *Hemingway: A Life without Consequences*, 390.

26. Ernest Hemingway, *Death in the Afternoon* (New York: Charles Scribner's Sons, 1932), 213. Reprinted with the permission of Scribner Publishing Group from DEATH IN THE AFTERNOON by Ernest Hemingway. Copyright © 1932 by Charles Scribner's Sons. Copyright renewed © 1960 by Ernest Hemingway. All rights reserved.

27. Ernest Hemingway, "The Snows of Kilimanjaro," in *The Snows of Kilimanjaro: And Other Stories* (New York: Charles Scribner's Sons, 1936), 9. Reprinted with the permission of Scribner Publishing Group from THE SNOWS OF KILIMANJARO: AND OTHER STORIES by Ernest Hemingway. Copyright © 1927 Charles Scribner's Sons; Copyright renewed 1955. 1927 Ernest Hemingway; Copyright renewed 1955. 1933 Charles Scribner's Sons; Copyright renewed 1961 by Ernest Hemingway. 1936 Ernest Hemingway; Copyright renewed 1964 by Mary Hemingway. All rights reserved.

28. Hemingway, "The Snows of Kilimanjaro," 9. Reprinted with the permission of Scribner Publishing Group from THE SNOWS OF KILI-MANJARO: AND OTHER STORIES by Ernest Hemingway. Copyright

29. Sanford, *At the Hemingways*, 20.

30. Ernest Hemingway, *Green Hills of Africa* (New York: Charles Scribner's Sons, 1935), 21.

31. John Chamberlain, *New York Times*, quoted in Mellow, *Hemingway: A Life without Consequences*, 440.

32. Marlene Dietrich, "The Most Fascinating Man I Know," *New York Herald Tribune*, February 13, 1955, 8–9.

33. Dietrich, "The Most Fascinating Man I Know," 8–9.

34. Ernest Hemingway, quoted in Dietrich, "The Most Fascinating Man I Know," 8–9.

35. Dietrich, "The Most Fascinating Man I Know," 8–9.

36. Dietrich, "The Most Fascinating Man I Know," 8–9.

37. Ernest Hemingway, Letter to Mike Strater, September 27, 1934, quoted in Paul Hendrickson, *Hemingway's Boat* (New York: Knopf, 2011), 74.

38. Ernest Hemingway, quoted in Mellow, *Hemingway: A Life without Consequences*, 485.

CHAPTER FOUR

1. Ernest Hemingway, Letter to the Pfeiffer Family, February 9, 1937, in *Ernest Hemingway: Selected Letters, 1917–1961*, ed. Carlos Baker (New York: Scribner's, 1981), 457.

2. Ernest Hemingway, Letter to Max Perkins, September 7, 1935, in *Ernest Hemingway: Selected Letters, 1917–1961*, 421.

SELECTED LETTERS 1917–1961 edited by Carlos Baker. Copyright ©
1981 by Carlos Baker and The Ernest Hemingway Foundation, Inc. All
rights reserved.

3. Ernest Hemingway, Letter to Ivan Kashkeen, January 12, 1936, in
Ernest Hemingway: Selected Letters, 1917–1961, 430. Reprinted with the
permission of Scribner Publishing Group from ERNEST HEMINGWAY,
SELECTED LETTERS 1917–1961 edited by Carlos Baker. Copyright ©
1981 by Carlos Baker and The Ernest Hemingway Foundation, Inc. All
rights reserved.

4. Ernest Hemingway, *To Have and Have Not* (New York: P.F. Collier
and Son, 1937), 28. Reprinted with the permission of Scribner Publishing
Group from TO HAVE AND HAVE NOT by Ernest Hemingway. Copyright © 1937 by Ernest Hemingway. Copyright renewed © 1965 by Mary
Hemingway. All rights reserved.

5. Hemingway, *To Have and Have Not*, 31. Reprinted with the permission of Scribner Publishing Group from TO HAVE AND HAVE NOT by
Ernest Hemingway. Copyright © 1937 by Ernest Hemingway. Copyright
renewed © 1965 by Mary Hemingway. All rights reserved.

6. Ernest Hemingway, *To Have and Have Not*, 240. Reprinted with the
permission of Scribner Publishing Group from TO HAVE AND HAVE
NOT by Ernest Hemingway. Copyright © 1937 by Ernest Hemingway.
Copyright renewed © 1965 by Mary Hemingway. All rights reserved.

7. Hemingway, *To Have and Have Not*, 232. Reprinted with the permission of Scribner Publishing Group from TO HAVE AND HAVE NOT
by Ernest Hemingway. Copyright © 1937 by Ernest Hemingway. Copyright renewed © 1965 by Mary Hemingway. All rights reserved.

8. Hemingway, *To Have and Have Not*, 225. Reprinted with the permission of Scribner Publishing Group from TO HAVE AND HAVE NOT
by Ernest Hemingway. Copyright © 1937 by Ernest Hemingway. Copyright renewed © 1965 by Mary Hemingway. All rights reserved.

9. Bernice Kert, *The Hemingway Women* (New York: Norton, 1983),
282.

10. Ernest Hemingway, "Mussolini, Europe's Prize Bluffer," in *Dateline: Toronto*, ed. W. White (New York: Charles Scribner's Sons, 1972),
253–59. Reprinted with the permission of Scribner Publishing Group
from ERNEST HEMINGWAY: DATELINE: TORONTO edited by William White. Copyright © 1985 by Mary Hemingway, John Hemingway,
Patrick Hemingway, and Gregory Hemingway. All rights reserved.

11. H. Matthews, quoted in John Raeburn, *Fame Became of Him:
Hemingway as a Public Writer* (Bloomington: Indiana University Press,
1984), 87.

12. Ernest Hemingway to Stephen Spender, quoted in J. Mellow, *Hemingway: A Life without Consequences* (New York: Addison-Wesley, 1992), 504.

13. Ernest Hemingway, "Hemingway Reports Spain," *The New Republic*, April 24, 1938, 350.

14. Ernest Hemingway, "Shelling of Madrid," *NANA Dispatch*, April 11, 1937, in *By-Line: Ernest Hemingway*, ed. W. White (New York: Charles Scribner's Sons, 1967), 259. Reprinted with the permission of Scribner Publishing Group from BY LINE: ERNEST HEMINGWAY edited by William White. Copyright © 1967 by By-Line Ernest Hemingway Inc. Copyright renewed © 1995 by Patrick Hemingway and John H. Hemingway. All rights reserved.

15. Hemingway, "Shelling of Madrid," in *By-Line*, 259. Reprinted with the permission of Scribner Publishing Group from BY LINE: ERNEST HEMINGWAY edited by William White. Copyright © 1967 by By-Line Ernest Hemingway Inc. Copyright renewed © 1995 by Patrick Hemingway and John H. Hemingway. All rights reserved.

16. Ernest Hemingway, "The Flight of the Refugees," *NANA Dispatch*, April 3, 1938, in *By-Line*, 281. Reprinted with the permission of Scribner Publishing Group from BY LINE: ERNEST HEMINGWAY edited by William White. Copyright © 1967 by By-Line Ernest Hemingway Inc. Copyright renewed © 1995 by Patrick Hemingway and John H. Hemingway. All rights reserved.

17. Ernest Hemingway, *A Farewell to Arms* (New York: Charles Scribner's Sons, 1929), 50. Reprinted with the permission of Scribner Publishing Group from A FAREWELL TO ARMS by Ernest Hemingway. Copyright © 1929 by Charles Scribner's Sons. Copyright renewed © 1957 by Ernest Hemingway. All rights reserved.

18. Ernest Hemingway, *For Whom the Bell Tolls* (New York: Charles Scribner's Sons, 1940), 467. Reprinted with the permission of Scribner Publishing Group from FOR WHOM THE BELL TOLLS by Ernest Hemingway. Copyright © 1940 by Ernest Hemingway. Copyright renewed © 1968 by Mary Hemingway. All rights reserved.

19. Ernest Hemingway to Carol Hemingway, 1945, quoted in Norberto Fuentes, *Hemingway in Cuba* (Secaucus, NJ: Lyle Stuart, 1984), 387–88.

20. Stephen Cooper, *The Politics of Ernest Hemingway* (Ann Arbor, MI: UMI Research Press, 1987), 118–19.

21. Ernest Hemingway, quoted in M. Reynolds, *The Final Years* (New York: Norton, 1999), 38.

22. A. E. Hotchner, *Hemingway and His World* (New York: Vendome Press), 136.

23. Ernest Hemingway, "Notes on the Next War: A Serious Topical Letter," *Esquire*, September 1935, in *By-Line*, 209. Reprinted with the permission of Scribner Publishing Group from BY LINE: ERNEST HEMINGWAY edited by William White. Copyright © 1967 by By-Line Ernest Hemingway Inc. Copyright renewed © 1995 by Patrick Hemingway and John H. Hemingway. All rights reserved.

24. Hemingway, "Notes on the Next War," in *By-Line*, 209. Reprinted with the permission of Scribner Publishing Group from BY LINE: ERNEST HEMINGWAY edited by William White. Copyright © 1967 by By-Line Ernest Hemingway Inc. Copyright renewed © 1995 by Patrick Hemingway and John H. Hemingway. All rights reserved.

25. Hemingway, "Notes on the Next War," in *By-Line*, 212. Reprinted with the permission of Scribner Publishing Group from BY LINE: ERNEST HEMINGWAY edited by William White. Copyright © 1967 by By-Line Ernest Hemingway Inc. Copyright renewed © 1995 by Patrick Hemingway and John H. Hemingway. All rights reserved.

26. Ernest Hemingway "Voyage to Victory," in *By-line*, 355. Reprinted with the permission of Scribner Publishing Group from BY LINE: ERNEST HEMINGWAY edited by William White. Copyright © 1967 by By-Line Ernest Hemingway Inc. Copyright renewed © 1995 by Patrick Hemingway and John H. Hemingway. All rights reserved.

27. Ernest Hemingway, quoted in Charles Whiting, *Hemingway Goes to War* (Gloucestershire, England: Sutton, 1999), 106.

28. Letter from David Bruce, 1947–1948, Hemingway Collection, John F. Kennedy Library, Boston, quoted in Hotchner, *Hemingway and His World*, 160.

29. Ernest Hemingway, quoted in Cooper, *The Politics of Ernest Hemingway*, 121.

30. Ernest Hemingway, quoted in Mary Welsh Hemingway, *How It Was* (New York: Alfred A. Knopf, 1976), 173.

CHAPTER FIVE

1. Ernest Hemingway to A. E. Hotchner, in Hotchner, *Hemingway and His World* (New York: Vendome Press, 1989), 199.

2. Ernest Hemingway, quoted in Hotchner, *Hemingway and His World*, 162.

3. Ernest Hemingway, quoted in Hotchner, *Hemingway and His World*, 162.

4. Jean-Paul Sartre, quoted in Ronald Hayman, *Sartre: A Biography* (New York: Simon & Schuster, 1987), 98.

5. Ernest Hemingway, Letter to Mary Welsh, August 1944, in *Ernest Hemingway: Selected Letters: 1917–1961*, ed. Carlos Baker (New York: Scribner's, 1981), 564–65. Reprinted with the permission of Scribner Publishing Group from ERNEST HEMINGWAY, SELECTED LETTERS 1917–1961 edited by Carlos Baker. Copyright © 1981 by Carlos Baker and The Ernest Hemingway Foundation, Inc. All rights reserved.

6. Ernest Hemingway, quoted in Mary Welsh Hemingway, *How It Was* (New York: Alfred A. Knopf, 1976), 108.

7. Ernest Hemingway, Letter to Hadley Mower, January 1938, in *Ernest Hemingway: Selected Letters: 1917–1961*, 463. Reprinted with the permission of Scribner Publishing Group from ERNEST HEMINGWAY, SELECTED LETTERS 1917–1961 edited by Carlos Baker. Copyright © 1981 by Carlos Baker and The Ernest Hemingway Foundation, Inc. All rights reserved.

8. Ernest Hemingway, Letter to Mrs. Paul Pfeiffer, January 1936, in *Ernest Hemingway: Selected Letters: 1917–1961*, 436. Reprinted with the permission of Scribner Publishing Group from ERNEST HEMINGWAY, SELECTED LETTERS 1917–1961 edited by Carlos Baker. Copyright © 1981 by Carlos Baker and The Ernest Hemingway Foundation, Inc. All rights reserved.

9. Ernest Hemingway, Letter to the Pfeiffer family, February 1937, in *Ernest Hemingway: Selected Letters: 1917–1961*, 457. Reprinted with the permission of Scribner Publishing Group from ERNEST HEMINGWAY, SELECTED LETTERS 1917–1961 edited by Carlos Baker. Copyright © 1981 by Carlos Baker and The Ernest Hemingway Foundation, Inc. All rights reserved.

10. Ernest Hemingway, Letter to Mary Welsh, quoted in J. Mellow, *Hemingway: A Life without Consequences* (New York: Addison-Wesley, 1992), 544.

11. Ernest Hemingway, Letter to Patrick Hemingway, in *Ernest Hemingway: Selected Letters: 1917–1961*, 576. Reprinted with the permission of Scribner Publishing Group from ERNEST HEMINGWAY, SELECTED LETTERS 1917–1961 edited by Carlos Baker. Copyright © 1981 by Carlos Baker and The Ernest Hemingway Foundation, Inc. All rights reserved.

12. Mary Welsh Hemingway, *How It Was*, 153.

13. Ernest Hemingway, Letter to Mary Welsh, quoted in Norberto Fuentes, *Hemingway in Cuba*, (Secaucus, NJ: Lyle Stuart, 1984), 353.

14. Grace Hall Hemingway, Letter to Ernest Hemingway, quoted in Mellow, *Hemingway: A Life without Consequences*, 546.

15. Ernest Hemingway, *Look*, 1956, quoted in Hotchner, *Hemingway and His World*, 167.

16. Ernest Hemingway, quoted in Hotchner, *Hemingway and His World*, 184.

17. Ernest Hemingway, Letter to Gary Cooper, March 1956, in *Ernest Hemingway: Selected Letters: 1917–1961*, 855. Reprinted with the permission of Scribner Publishing Group from ERNEST HEMINGWAY, SELECTED LETTERS 1917–1961 edited by Carlos Baker. Copyright © 1981 by Carlos Baker and The Ernest Hemingway Foundation, Inc. All rights reserved.

18. Ernest Hemingway, Letter to Patrick Hemingway, *Ernest Hemingway: Selected Letters 1917–1961*, 576. Reprinted with the permission of Scribner Publishing Group from ERNEST HEMINGWAY, SELECTED LETTERS 1917–1961 edited by Carlos Baker. Copyright © 1981 by Carlos Baker and The Ernest Hemingway Foundation, Inc. All rights reserved.

19. Ernest Hemingway, Letter to Mrs. Paul Pfeiffer, February 1939, in *Ernest Hemingway: Selected Letters: 1917–1961*, 478. Reprinted with the permission of Scribner Publishing Group from ERNEST HEMINGWAY, SELECTED LETTERS 1917–1961 edited by Carlos Baker. Copyright © 1981 by Carlos Baker and The Ernest Hemingway Foundation, Inc. All rights reserved.

20. Ernest Hemingway, Letter to Mrs. Paul Pfeiffer, January 1936, in *Ernest Hemingway: Selected Letters: 1917–1961*, 434. Reprinted with the permission of Scribner Publishing Group from ERNEST HEMINGWAY, SELECTED LETTERS 1917–1961 edited by Carlos Baker. Copyright © 1981 by Carlos Baker and The Ernest Hemingway Foundation, Inc. All rights reserved.

21. Ernest Hemingway, Letter to Mrs. Paul Pfeiffer, January 1936, *Ernest Hemingway: Selected Letters: 1917–1961*, 434. Reprinted with the permission of Scribner Publishing Group from ERNEST HEMINGWAY, SELECTED LETTERS 1917–1961 edited by Carlos Baker. Copyright © 1981 by Carlos Baker and The Ernest Hemingway Foundation, Inc. All rights reserved.

22. Martha Gellhorn, Letter to Hadley Mower, quoted in Hotchner, *Hemingway and His World*, 151.

23. Patrick Hemingway, quoted in Hotchner, *Hemingway and His World*, 169.

24. Gregory Hemingway, quoted in Hotchner, *Hemingway and His World*, 129.

25. Ernest Hemingway, Reproduced Letter to Peter Viertel, March 10, 1948, Paul Newman Collection, San Francisco.

26. Mary Welsh Hemingway, *How It Was*, 323.

27. Adriana Ivancich, quoted in Bernice Kert, *The Hemingway Women* (New York: W. W. Norton, 1983), 450–51.

28. Adriana Ivancich, quoted in Kert, *The Hemingway Women*, 443.

29. Mary Welsh Hemingway, *How It Was*, 283

30. Kert, *The Hemingway Women*, 456.

31. M. Geismar, *Saturday Review of Literature*, quoted in Mellow, *Hemingway: A Life without Consequences*, 560.

32. Guido Guerrara, "Hemingway the Hunter," Paper presented at Fourteenth Ernest Hemingway Colloquium, Havana, June 2013.

33. Ernest Hemingway, *Conversations with Ernest Hemingway*, ed. M. Bruccoli (Jackson: University Press of Mississippi, 1986), 61–62.

34. Ernest Hemingway, quoted in C. Baker, "Introduction," *Hemingway and His Critics* (New York: Hill and Wang, 1961), 10.

35. Ernest Hemingway, *The Old Man and the Sea* (New York: Charles Scribner's Sons, 1952), 103. Reprinted with the permission of Scribner Publishing Group from THE OLD MAN AND THE SEA by Ernest Hemingway. Copyright © 1952 by Ernest Hemingway. Copyright renewed © 1980 by Mary Hemingway. All rights reserved.

36. Mark Schorer, *The New Republic*, quoted in Mellow, *Hemingway: A Life without Consequences*, 581.

37. Orville Prescott, *New York Times*, quoted in Mellow, *Hemingway: A Life without Consequences*, 581.

38. Fidel Castro, quoted in M. Reynolds, *The Final Years* (New York: Norton, 1999), 323.

39. Mary Welsh Hemingway, *How It Was*, 527–28.

40. Mary Welsh Hemingway, *How It Was*, 564.

41. Mary Welsh Hemingway, *How It Was*, 565.

Chapter Six

1. Ernest Hemingway, "Indian Camp" (1925), in *The Nick Adam Stories* (New York: Charles Scribner's Sons, 1972), 19. Reprinted with the permission of Scribner Publishing Group from THE NICK ADAMS

STORIES by Ernest Hemingway. Copyright © 1972 and renewed © 2000 by The Ernest Hemingway Foundation. All rights reserved.

2. Ernest Hemingway, Letter to Gianfranco Ivancich, January 7, 1959, in *Ernest Hemingway: Selected Letters: 1917–1961*, ed. Carlos Baker (New York: Scribner's, 1981), 890–91. Reprinted with the permission of Scribner Publishing Group from ERNEST HEMINGWAY, SELECTED LETTERS 1917–1961 edited by Carlos Baker. Copyright © 1981 by Carlos Baker and The Ernest Hemingway Foundation, Inc. All rights reserved.

3. Ernest Hemingway, Reproduction of Letter to Peter Viertel, June 10, 1948, Paul Newman Collection, San Francisco.

4. Ernest Hemingway, Reproduction of Letter to Peter Viertel, November 12, 1948, Paul Newman Collection, San Francisco.

5. Ernest Hemingway to Patrick Hemingway, November 24, 1958, in *Ernest Hemingway: Selected Letters: 1917–1961*, 887–88. Reprinted with the permission of Scribner Publishing Group from ERNEST HEMINGWAY, SELECTED LETTERS 1917–1961 edited by Carlos Baker. Copyright © 1981 by Carlos Baker and The Ernest Hemingway Foundation, Inc. All rights reserved.

6. Ernest Hemingway to J. F. Kennedy, January 24, 1961, in *Ernest Hemingway: Selected Letters: 1917–1961*, 916. Reprinted with the permission of Scribner Publishing Group from ERNEST HEMINGWAY, SELECTED LETTERS 1917–1961 edited by Carlos Baker. Copyright © 1981 by Carlos Baker and The Ernest Hemingway Foundation, Inc. All rights reserved.

7. Ernest Hemingway to Max Perkins, January 8, 1929, *Ernest Hemingway: Selected Letters: 1917–1961*, 292. Reprinted with the permission of Scribner Publishing Group from ERNEST HEMINGWAY, SELECTED LETTERS 1917–1961 edited by Carlos Baker. Copyright © 1981 by Carlos Baker and The Ernest Hemingway Foundation, Inc. All rights reserved.

8. Spruille Braden, *Diplomats and Demagogues* (New York: Arlington House, 1971), 282–84.

9. D. M. Ladd, Letter to J. Edgar Hoover, December 17, 1942, vault. FBI.gov/ernest-miller-hemingway (accessed June 11, 2013).

10. Ladd, Letter to J. Edgar Hoover, December 17, 1942.

11. Ernest Hemingway, Letter to L. H. Brague, January 24, 1959, in *Ernest Hemingway: Selected Letters: 1917–1961*, 892. Reprinted with the permission of Scribner Publishing Group from ERNEST HEMINGWAY, SELECTED LETTERS 1917–1961 edited by Carlos Baker. Copyright © 1981 by Carlos Baker and The Ernest Hemingway Foundation, Inc. All rights reserved.

12. E. Hemingway, quoted in M. Reynolds, *Hemingway: The Final Years* (New York: Norton, 1999), 335.

13. Ernest Hemingway, Letter to Mrs. Paul Pfieffer, January 26, 1936, in *Ernest Hemingway: Selected Letters: 1917–1961*, 435–36. Reprinted with the permission of Scribner Publishing Group from ERNEST HEMINGWAY, SELECTED LETTERS 1917–1961 edited by Carlos Baker. Copyright © 1981 by Carlos Baker and The Ernest Hemingway Foundation, Inc. All rights reserved.

14. Mary Welsh Hemingway, *How It Was* (New York: Alfred A. Knopf, 1976), 568.

15. Ernest Hemingway, Letter to H. Breit, February 4, 1954, in *Ernest Hemingway: Selected Letters: 1917–1961*, 829. Reprinted with the permission of Scribner Publishing Group from ERNEST HEMINGWAY, SELECTED LETTERS 1917–1961 edited by Carlos Baker. Copyright © 1981 by Carlos Baker and The Ernest Hemingway Foundation, Inc. All rights reserved.

16. E. M. Halliday, "Hemingway's Ambiguity: Symbolism and Irony," *American Literature* 28 (March 1956): 3.

17. Ernest Hemingway, Letter to Bill and Bunny Horne, July 1958, in *Ernest Hemingway: Selected Letters: 1917–1961*, 884. Reprinted with the permission of Scribner Publishing Group from ERNEST HEMINGWAY, SELECTED LETTERS 1917–1961 edited by Carlos Baker. Copyright © 1981 by Carlos Baker and The Ernest Hemingway Foundation, Inc. All rights reserved.

18. G. Plimpton, "An Interview with Ernest Hemingway," in *Hemingway and His Critics*, ed. Carlos Baker (New York: Hill and Wang, 1961), 24.

19. Ernest Hemingway, *Death in the Afternoon* (New York: Charles Scribner's Sons, 1932), 122. Reprinted with the permission of Scribner Publishing Group from DEATH IN THE AFTERNOON by Ernest Hemingway. Copyright © 1932 by Charles Scribner's Sons. Copyright renewed © 1960 by Ernest Hemingway. All rights reserved.

20. Ernest Hemingway, quoted in Carlos Baker, *Ernest Hemingway: A Life Story* (New York: Charles Scribner's Sons, 1969), 366.

21. Ernest Hemingway to Wallace Meyer, February 1952, quoted in J. Mellow, *Hemingway: A Life without Consequences* (New York: Addison-Wesley, 1992), 550.

22. Ernest Hemingway to Carlos Baker, quoted in Mellow, *Hemingway: A Life without Consequences*, 572.

23. Mary Welsh Hemingway, quoted in A. E. Hotchner, *Hemingway and His World* (New York: Vendome Press, 1989), 200.

24. Ernest Hemingway to Malcolm Crowley, September 1945, quoted in Mellow, *Hemingway: A Life without Consequences*, 549.

25. M. Reynolds, *The Final Years*, 350.

26. Mary Welsh Hemingway, *How It Was*, 500–502.

CHAPTER SEVEN

1. Gertrude Stein, *The Autobiography of Alice B. Toklas* (New York: Harcourt Brace & Company, 1933), 266.

2. Bill Horne, quoted in Virginia Moseley, "Hemingway Remembered," *Barrington Courier Review*, September 27, 1979, 28–33.

3. Leicester Hemingway, *My Brother, Ernest Hemingway* (Cleveland: World, 1962), 14–16.

4. Stein, *The Autobiography of Alice B. Toklas*, 266.

5. William Shakespeare, *Henry IV, Part 2*, quoted in "The Short Happy Life of Francis Macomber," 150.

6. Ernest Hemingway, *To Have and Have Not* (New York: P.F. Collier and Son, 1937), 225. Reprinted with the permission of Scribner Publishing Group from TO HAVE AND HAVE NOT by Ernest Hemingway. Copyright © 1937 by Ernest Hemingway. Copyright renewed © 1965 by Mary Hemingway. All rights reserved.

7. John Donne, *Mediations XVII*, quoted in Ernest Hemingway, *For Whom the Bell Tolls* (New York: Charles Scribner's Sons, 1940), title and preface.

8. Stonewall Jackson, quoted in "The Mighty Stonewall," www.con federatelegion.com/The_Mighty_Stonewall.html (accessed July 24, 2013).

9. Marcelline Hemingway Sanford, *At the Hemingways* (Moscow: University of Idaho Press), 135.

10. *The Holy Bible*, Ecclesiastes 1:4–5.

11. Ernest Hemingway, quoted in George Plimpton, "An Interview with Hemingway," *Hemingway and His Critics*, ed. Carlos Baker (New York: Hill and Wang, 1961), 29.

12. Ernest Hemingway, *The Old Man and the Sea* (New York: Charles Scribner's Sons, 1952), 107. Reprinted with the permission of Scribner Publishing Group from THE OLD MAN AND THE SEA by Ernest Hemingway. Copyright © 1952 by Ernest Hemingway. Copyright renewed © 1980 by Mary Hemingway. All rights reserved.

13. Hemingway, *The Old Man and the Sea*, 10. Reprinted with the permission of Scribner Publishing Group from THE OLD MAN AND THE

14. Hemingway, *The Old Man and the Sea*, 57.

15. Hemingway, *The Old Man and the Sea*, 121.

16. Hemingway, *The Old Man and the Sea*, 122.

17. Hemingway, *The Old Man and the Sea*, 103.

18. Ernest Hemingway, *A Farewell to Arms* (New York: Charles Scribner's Sons, 1929), 232.

19. Hemingway, *A Farewell to Arms*, 284.

20. *Kansas City Star Style Sheet*, www.kansascity.com/2007/07/29/210322/istar-style-rules-for-writing.html (accessed July 20, 2013).

21. Sheridan Baker, *Ernest Hemingway: An Introduction and Interpretation* (Ann Arbor: University of Michigan, 1967), 10.

22. Hemingway, quoted in George Plimpton, "An Interview with Hemingway," in *Hemingway and His Critics*, 34.

23. Hemingway, quoted in Plimpton, "Interview with Hemingway," in *Hemingway and His Critics*, 34.

24. Ernest Hemingway, Letter to Clarence Hemingway, March 20, 1925, in *Ernest Hemingway: Selected Letters: 1917–1961*, ed. Carlos Baker (New York: Scribner's, 1981), 153.

25. Sanford, *At the Hemingways*, 219.

26. Stein, *The Autobiography of Alice B. Toklas*, 266.

27. Ernest Hemingway, Letter to Ezra Pound, July 22, 1933, quoted in J. Mellow, *Hemingway: A Life without Consequences* (New York: Addison-Wesley, 1992), 423.

28. Joseph Wood Krutch, *The Nation*, quoted in Mellow, *Hemingway: A Life without Consequences*, 355.

29. Sanford, *At the Hemingways*, 184.

30. Audre Hannaman, quoted in Mellow, *Hemingway: A Life without Consequences*, 334–35.

31. Stephen Cooper, *The Politics of Ernest Hemingway* (Ann Arbor, MI: UMI Research Press, 1987), 49.

32. Ernest Hemingway, Letter to Paul Romaine, July 6, 1932, in *Ernest Hemingway: Selected Letters: 1917–1961*, 363. Reprinted with the permission of Scribner Publishing Group from ERNEST HEMINGWAY, SELECTED LETTERS 1917–1961 edited by Carlos Baker. Copyright © 1981 by Carlos Baker and The Ernest Hemingway Foundation, Inc. All rights reserved.

33. Hemingway, *To Have and Have Not*, 225. Reprinted with the permission of Scribner Publishing Group from TO HAVE AND HAVE NOT by Ernest Hemingway. Copyright © 1937 by Ernest Hemingway. Copyright renewed © 1965 by Mary Hemingway. All rights reserved.

34. Hemingway, *For Whom the Bell Tolls*, introduction. Reprinted with the permission of Scribner Publishing Group from FOR WHOM THE BELL TOLLS by Ernest Hemingway. Copyright © 1940 by Ernest Hemingway. Copyright renewed © 1968 by Mary Hemingway. All rights reserved.

35. Ernest Hemingway, *Green Hills of Africa* (New York: Charles Scribner's Sons, 1935), 191. Reprinted with the permission of Scribner Publishing Group from GREEN HILLS OF AFRICA by Ernest Hemingway. Copyright © 1935 by Charles Scribner's Sons. Copyright renewed © 1963 by Mary Hemingway. All rights reserved.

36. Hemingway, *Green Hills of Africa*, 191. Reprinted with the permission of Scribner Publishing Group from GREEN HILLS OF AFRICA by Ernest Hemingway. Copyright © 1935 by Charles Scribner's Sons. Copyright renewed © 1963 by Mary Hemingway. All rights reserved.

37. Thomas Putnam, "Hemingway on War and Its Aftermath," The National Archives, www.archives.gov/publications/prologue/2006/spring/hemingway.html (accessed July 27, 2013).

38. John O'Hara, "The Author's Name Is Hemingway," *New York Times Book Review*, September 10, 1950, 1, 30.

39. Eliot Paul, *Providence Sunday Journal*, September 10, 1950, vi–8.

40. Alfred Kazin, "The Indignant Flesh," *The New Yorker*, September 19, 1950, 113–18.

41. Hemingway, *The Old Man and the Sea*, 103. Reprinted with the permission of Scribner Publishing Group from THE OLD MAN AND THE SEA by Ernest Hemingway. Copyright © 1952 by Ernest Hemingway. Copyright renewed © 1980 by Mary Hemingway. All rights reserved.

42. Ernest Hemingway, Nobel Prize Acceptance Speech, www.Nobel Prize.org/nobel_prizes/literature/laureates/1954/hemingway-speech.html (accessed July 20, 2013).

43. Ernest Hemingway, quoted in Plimpton, "An Interview with Ernest Hemingway," in *Hemingway and His Critics*, 22.

44. Hemingway, Nobel Prize Acceptance Speech.

Bibliography

Baker, Carlos. *Ernest Hemingway: A Life Story*. New York: Charles Scribner's Sons, 1969.

———, ed. *Hemingway and His Critics*. New York: Hill and Wang, 1961.

Baker, Milford. *Milford Baker Diary*, June 7, 1918. Carlos Baker papers.

Baker, Sheridan. *Ernest Hemingway: An Introduction and Interpretation*. Ann Arbor: University of Michigan, 1967.

Biggs, Fannie. *Memories of Ernest Hemingway*. Charles Fenton Papers, February 24, 1952. Yale Collection of American Literature, Beinecke Rare Book Room and Manuscript Library, Yale University.

Braden, Spruille. *Diplomats and Demagogues*. New York: Arlington House, 1971.

Cooper, Stephen. *The Politics of Ernest Hemingway*. Ann Arbor, MI: UMI Research Press, 1987.

Dietrich, Marlene. "The Most Fascinating Man I Know." *New York Herald Tribune*, February 13, 1955, 8–9.

Donnelly, H., and R. Billings. *Sara & Gerald*. New York: Times Books, 1982.

Fuentes, Norberto. *Hemingway in Cuba*. Secaucus, NJ: Lyle Stuart, 1984.

Griffin, Peter. *Along with Youth*. New York: Oxford University Press, 1985.

Guerrara, Guido. "Hemingway the Hunter." Paper presented at the Fourteenth Ernest Hemingway Colloquium, Havana, June 2013.

Halliday, E. M. "Hemingway's Ambiguity: Symbolism and Irony." *American Literature* 28 (March 1956): 3.

Hayman, Ronald. *Sartre: A Biography*. New York: Simon & Schuster. 1987.

Hemingway, Anson. *Civil War Journal*. May 1863. Special Collections, Oak Park Public Library, Oak Park, Illinois.

Hemingway, Clarence. Letters to Ernest Hemingway. July 29, 1915; April 17, 1918; July 17, 1918; June 4, 1928. Hemingway Collection, John F. Kennedy Library, Boston.

Hemingway, Ernest. "American Bohemians in Paris." In *Dateline: Toronto*, ed. W. White, 114–15. New York: Charles Scribner's Sons, 1985.

——. *By-Line: Ernest Hemingway*. Ed. W. White. New York: Charles Scribner's Sons, 1967.

——. "Clemenceau Politically Dead." In *Dateline: Toronto*, ed. W. White, 94. New York: Charles Scribner's Sons, 1985.

——. *Conversations with Ernest Hemingway*. Ed. Matthew Bruccoli. Jackson: University Press of Mississippi, 1986.

——. *Death in the Afternoon*. New York: Charles Scribner's Sons, 1932.

——. *Ernest Hemingway: Selected Letters: 1917–1961*. Ed. Carlos Baker. New York: Scribner's, 1981.

——. *A Farewell to Arms*. New York: Charles Scribner's Sons, 1929.

——. *For Whom the Bell Tolls*. New York: Charles Scribner's Sons, 1940.

——. *Green Hills of Africa*. New York: Charles Scribner's Sons, 1935.

——, quoted in "Hemingway Here, Avid for Lion Hunt." *New York Times*, April 4, 1934. www.nytimes.com/books.99/07/04/specials/hemingway-lionhunt.html (accessed June 22, 2012).

——. "Hemingway Reports Spain." *The New Republic* 94, April 24, 1938.

——. *In Our Time*. New York: Charles Scribner's Sons, 1925.

——. Letter to Bill Horne. March 13, 1919. Ernest Hemingway Foundation of Oak Park Collection.

——. *A Moveable Feast*. New York: Charles Scribner's Sons, 1964.

——. "Mussolini, Europe's Prize Bluffer." In *Dateline: Toronto*, ed. W. White, 253–59. New York: Charles Scribner's Sons, 1985.

——. *The Nick Adams Stories*. New York: Charles Scribner's Sons, 1972.

——. Nobel Prize Acceptance Speech. www.NobelPrize.org/nobel_prizes/literature/laureates/1954/hemingway-speech.html (accessed July 20, 2013).

——. *The Old Man and the Sea*. New York: Charles Scribner's Sons, 1952.

——. Selected Letters to Peter Viertel. Reproductions, Paul Newman Collection, San Francisco.

——. "A Silent, Ghastly Procession." In *Dateline: Toronto*, ed. W. White, 232. New York: Charles Scribner's Sons, 1985.

——. "The Snows of Kilimanjaro." In *The Snows of Kilimanjaro: And Other Stories*. New York: Charles Scribner's Sons, 1936.

———. *The Sun Also Rises*. New York: Charles Scribner's Sons, 1926.

———. *Three Stories and Ten Poems*. Paris: Contact Publishing, 1923.

———. *To Have and Have Not*. New York: P.F. Collier and Son, 1937.

———. *The Trapeze*. Oak Park: Oak Park High School, 1916.

———. "Try Bobsledding if You Want Thrills." In *Dateline: Toronto*, ed. W. White, 101–2. New York: Charles Scribner's Sons, 1985.

Hemingway, Grace Hall. Letter to Ernest Hemingway. April 17, 1918. Hemingway Collection, John F. Kennedy Library, Boston.

———. *Memory Book I*. Hemingway Collection, John F. Kennedy Library, Boston.

Hemingway, Leicester. *My Brother, Ernest Hemingway*. Cleveland: World, 1962.

Hemingway, Mary Welsh. *How It Was*. New York: Alfred A. Knopf, 1976.

Hendrickson, Paul. *Hemingway's Boat*. New York: Knopf, 2011.

Holy Bible. Nashville, TN: National Publishing Company, 1961.

Hotchner, A. E. *Hemingway and His World*. New York: Vendome Press, 1989.

Jackson, Stonewall, quoted in "The Mighty Stonewall." www.confeder atelegion.com/The_Mighty_Stonewall.html (accessed July 24, 2013).

Kansas City Star Style Sheet. www.kansascity.com/2007/07/29/210322/ istar-style-rules-for-writing.html (accessed July 20, 2013).

Kazin, Alfred. "The Indignant Flesh." *The New Yorker*, September 19, 1950, 113–18.

Kert, Bernice. *The Hemingway Women*. New York: W. W. Norton, 1983.

Ladd, D. M. Letter to J. Edgar Hoover. December 17, 1942. vault.FBI .gov/ernest-miller-hemingway.

Lewis, Robert. "Hemingway in Italy." *Journal of Modern Literature* (May 1982): 215.

Lynn, Kenneth. *Hemingway*. New York: Simon and Schuster, 1987.

Mellow, J. *Hemingway: A Life without Consequences*. New York: Addison-Wesley, 1992.

Montessori, Maria, quoted in "Maria Montessori Quotes." *Daily Montessori*, 2011. www.dailymontessori.com/maria-montessori-quotes/ (accessed June 21, 2012).

Moseley, Virginia. "Hemingway Remembered." *Barrington Courier Review*, September 27, 1979, 28–33.

Nickel, Matthew. "Young Hemingway's Wound and Conversion." *Pilgrim*, March 2013, 1–13.

O'Hara, John. "The Author's Name Is Hemingway." *New York Times Book Review*, September 10, 1950, 1, 30.

Paul, Eliot. *Providence Sunday Journal*, September 10, 1950, vi–8.

Platt, Frank. "Hemingway's Oak Park Years." Panel Discussion at Triton College, River Grove, Illinois, September 24, 1974.

Plimpton, G. "An Interview with Ernest Hemingway." In *Hemingway and His Critics*, ed. Carlos Baker. New York: Hill and Wang, 1961.

Putnam, Thomas. "Hemingway on War and Its Aftermath." The National Archives. www.archives.gov/publications/prologue/2006/spring/hemingway.html (accessed July 27, 2013).

Raeburn, John. *Fame Became of Him: Hemingway as a Public Writer*. Bloomington: Indiana University Press, 1984.

Reynolds, M. *The Final Years*. New York: Norton, 1999.

———. *The Paris Years*. Cambridge, MA: Basil Blackwell, 1980.

Sanford, Marcelline. *At the Hemingways*. Moscow: University of Idaho Press, 1999.

Shakespeare, William. *Henry IV, Part 2, Shakespeare: The Complete Works*. Ed. G. B. Harrison. New York: Harcourt Brace, 1952.

Stein, Gertrude. *The Autobiography of Alice B. Toklas*. New York: Harcourt Brace & Company, 1933.

Villard, H., and Nagel, J. *Hemingway in Love and War: The Lost Diary of Agnes Von Kurowsky*. Boston: Northeastern University Press, 1989.

von Kurowsky, Agnes. Letter to Ernest Hemingway. March 7, 1919. Ernest Hemingway Foundation of Oak Park Collection, Oak Park, Illinois.

Whiting, Charles. *Hemingway Goes to War*. Gloucestershire, England: Sutton, 1999.

Young, Philip. *Ernest Hemingway: A Reconsideration*. New York: Harcourt, Brace & World, 1966.

Index

About the Author

Nancy W. Sindelar has spent more than thirty years in education as a teacher, administrator, university professor, and consultant and has published numerous articles and three books on educational topics. Her interest in Hemingway was nurtured as she taught American literature at Oak Park and River Forest High School, Hemingway's alma mater, and as a thirty-two-year resident of Oak Park River Forest, Hemingway's home from birth until his departure for Kansas City after graduation from high school.

Currently, Dr. Sindelar is a board member of the Ernest Hemingway Foundation of Oak Park and has supported numerous Hemingway functions and made many popular presentations about the life and work of Ernest Hemingway. In June 2011 and 2013, she made presentations at the International Ernest Hemingway Colloquium in Havana, Cuba, and has been invited to speak at the Hemingway Society Conference in Venice in 2014. In addition to working with private organizations, libraries, and book clubs interested in learning more about the life of Ernest Hemingway, Sindelar teaches Hemingway: The Man, The Writer, The Legend at the University of California, Riverside. She holds a B.S. in English, M.A. in literature, C.A.S. in educational administration, and Ph.D. in educational leadership and policy studies.